RAISING GRITTY KIDS

raising gritty kids

YOUR GUIDE TO PARENTING IN TIMES OF UNCERTAINTY

KARA YOKLEY

WITH HER MOTHER

CONSTANCE YOKLEY

COPYRIGHT © 2021 KARA YOKLEY & CONSTANCE YOKLEY
All rights reserved.

RAISING GRITTY KIDS
Your Guide to Parenting in Times of Uncertainty

ISBN   978-1-5445-1861-9 *Hardcover*
         978-1-5445-1860-2 *Paperback*
         978-1-5445-1859-6 *Ebook*

TO A BETTER WORLD

Contents

INTRODUCTION 9

1. KNOW THE LANDSCAPE 23

2. KNOW YOUR CHILD 49

3. NURTURING MENTAL INTERESTS.................................. 71

4. PHYSICALITY AND SELF-ESTEEM.................................. 91

5. DEVELOPING AN EMOTIONAL TOOL KIT 109

6. DEVELOPING SOCIAL PRESENCE IN A SHIFTING LANDSCAPE ... 129

7. NURTURING SPIRITUALITY AND ETHICAL BEHAVIOR 147

8. MONEY AND RAISING RESILIENT KIDS...................... 159

9. DON'T LOSE YOURSELF IN YOUR PARENTING 177

10. PARENTING WITH OTHERS 191

11. READY TO LAUNCH 215

CONCLUSION.. 231

ACKNOWLEDGMENTS... 235

ABOUT THE AUTHORS 237

NOTES 239

Introduction

She doesn't talk much about the war days, but when she does, I listen, rapt with attention. My husband's grandmother came of age during World War II. Spend any amount of time with her today, and you can't help but be struck by her strength and zest for life.

It can be hard to imagine growing up in a landscape shaped by such upheaval. And yet, life goes on. Babcia married, had children who had children, lived through the loss of a husband and a child. She left her home in search of a better life, watched the world become more interconnected and then more digital, and through it all, carried on—through all the dramas, large and small, personal and impersonal, mundane and heartbreaking. Her fearlessness and resilience in the face of change seem to be the precise result of having lived through so many changes.

In reality, each of us will live through many personal and societal upheavals. When I first conceived of this book project with my mom, I never could have anticipated the circumstances under which we would be writing. Truly, these are extraordinary times. Who knew the rapidity with which the COVID-19 crisis would unfold and that day-to-day life would change so dramatically? That we would witness a frightening reinforcement of old anxieties around money and tribalism? How could we have known there would be an immediate need to reassess the extent and nature of personal freedoms?

I have lived through my share of personal upheaval. So, even before COVID-19, I made every effort to be flexible in my thinking and adaptable in my actions. However, the sweeping nature of the pandemic took me by surprise and forced me to reflect anew on the need for resilience in the face of unforeseen challenges.

In this book, my mother and I hope to share ideas and reflections that are relevant today, perhaps now even more so than before. COVID-19 has been a wake-up call. Ultimately, decisions made halfway around the world affected everyone's ability to work, educate and learn, exercise, shop, travel, and simply be in the company of others. This uncertain environment has caused many to question how much anybody truly understands the world in which we live. As parents, this reality can be especially daunting.

Most parents feel the weight of responsibility to protect their children, to do what is best for them, to help them launch into adulthood, and to achieve success. Yet in these uncertain times, the best way to do that is often unclear. These current challenges underscore the anxieties many American parents already felt as they looked to the future—the prohibitive cost of higher education, the mismatch between salaries and childcare costs, the escalating price of home ownership and cost of living. In the context of today's landscape, these age-old questions only add to the intensity of felt anxieties.

Brené Brown has said, "Ironically, parenting is a shame and judgment minefield precisely because most of us are wading through uncertainty and self-doubt when it comes to raising our children."[1] The natural instinct of most parents is to help their children thrive. It is a biological imperative. However, here's the thing: the model that worked for past generations seems to be broken, and it feels hard to carve out something new.

America is in a period of flux and there is a lot about which to be anxious. How does one prepare children for the future when the paths to success are no longer clear? How is one to raise well-balanced, productive, resilient members of society who can handle whatever life throws at them? Goodness knows, a lot could be coming their way.

This book offers a practical framework to help answer these questions. Our intent is not to suggest one definitive way to parent. Rather, we are providing research-backed tools to help you identify and refine your parenting style and to develop the best plan for *your* child in *your* landscape, a plan that will give you confidence that you are indeed making the best choices possible for your unique situation.

ORGANIC PARENTING

Shinichi Suzuki came of age at a time of great global upheaval. In many ways, those profound experiences shaped him into a true citizen of the world and influenced the music education philosophy he would later develop. In *Nurtured by Love*,

INTRODUCTION · 11

Suzuki says, "Our aim needs to be the nurturing of children. The moment we rigidly convince ourselves, 'Education is what we're after,' we warp a child's development. First foster the heart, then help the child acquire ability. This is indeed nature's proper way."[2]

Organic parenting takes into consideration some of Suzuki's revelations. Instead of a rigid set of rules, we offer a framework that focuses on fostering your child's heart and spirit and helping your child acquire the ability to navigate the changes and uncertainties of life.

The framework is grounded in two basic principles:

1. Knowing the present and shifting social, familial, and cultural landscape in which you are raising your child
2. Knowing your child's interests, preferences, personality, strengths and weaknesses, and more

Organic parenting is responsive. It respects the individuality of each child and does not compare siblings or peers, so as not to inadvertently impose on one child the expectations had for another. It does not mean leaving a child to his own devices. It means allowing the child to make age-appropriate decisions and being ready to offer guidance as a wise observer-participant.

From this vantage point, it is possible to craft decisions with confidence derived from knowing that the unique landscape and the characteristics of the child have been fully considered.

In the pages that follow, we discuss various aspects of this framework along with concrete suggestions for applying it within your environment:

- In chapter 1, we discuss the first principle: understanding the landscape in which you are raising your child, shifting and uncertain as it may be.
- In chapter 2, we discuss what it means to know your child and to make parenting decisions based on his unique characteristics.
- In chapters 3–7, we look more closely at five aspects of your child's makeup and the landscape in which she lives: mental, physical, emotional, social, and ethical/spiritual. We also present ideas for developing and navigating each component in a way that makes sense for your child. Think of your home as a safe place in which your child can try on and practice new skillsets that will help her function responsibly in the real world.
- In chapter 8, we delve into money and how it relates to raising resilient children.
- In chapter 9, we suggest ways to embrace the opportunities for personal growth that parenting provides, without losing yourself entirely in your parenting.
- In chapter 10, we discuss challenges that arise as you parent with others. We provide suggestions for harmoniously navigating the wishes and quirks of partners, grandparents, teachers, and more in ways that benefit your child.
- In chapter 11, we provide suggestions for laying the groundwork for your child's eventual launch into adulthood.

Four important threads weave in and out of our framework, as well as each chapter: love, respect, trust, and curiosity. Out of a foundation of love for one's child comes respect for his individuality and personhood. Through conversation and mutual engagement, trust is born, which creates a healthy parent-

INTRODUCTION · 13

child relationship. Finally, to parent organically, one has to be curious about the current landscape, to ask questions and embark on a quest to find the path that makes the most sense given the landscape and the child. You remain your child's first model of love, respect, trust, curiosity—and resiliency.

My mom and I talked at length about the kinds of new choices we observed parents making today. In this book, my mom shares generously her own experience with the organic parenting method. In the main text, I discuss her method, tips on applying the framework, and resources for more information. Each chapter also features sidebars penned by my mom, Connie. These stories illustrate principles from the main text through family history, glimpses of cultural landscape, and examples of organic parenting in action. Later in this introduction, for example, Connie explains how and why her organic parenting style came to be.

COMING OF AGE ON THE SOUTHSIDE OF CHICAGO

Much as is the case in families everywhere, my two siblings and I exhibited different personality traits from the start. In our little home, there was no shortage of sibling drama. My older sister was strong, one might dare say, headstrong. Once Nora decided how things were going to go—be it what clothes she wanted to wear, what after-school activities she wanted to pursue, or getting married at age nineteen and sneaking out to elope if my parents didn't agree—woe to anyone who got in her way. She was dedicated to her principles in a way that made her unafraid to engage in all-out combat to get her way.

From the get-go, my younger brother was the cool one. He had an ease with peers and grownups alike that I often

14 · RAISING GRITTY KIDS

watched with a tinge of envy. He had some natural-born Jedi mind tricks that made argument and debate unnecessary. He had my parents indulging him with whole trays of cinnamon rolls and seemingly endless episodes of *DuckTales* and *Gumby*. David was that rare child who was simultaneously brilliant and popular, nerdy and cool. Both captain of the math club and his youth soccer team, he flitted between groups like it was no big deal. And yet, he was most comfortable close to home.

As the middle child, I craved acceptance and approval. Sure, I had my moments of pushing boundaries, like the time when I was seven and decided to cut choir practice to hang out with the "naughty" kids because I wanted to walk on the wild side (i.e., play on the swings behind the church). Generally, though, one stern look from my mother was all it took to have me quivering in my boots. I was nerdy and plump, intensely competitive, and awkward all at once. More than anything, however, I was curious about the world. I had a sense that there was so much more to experience beyond the confines of our little neighborhood. For as long as I can remember, I've always been on the lookout for my next big adventure.

Today, my sister lives in a deeply conservative environment in the southeastern United States. Nora is an evangelical minister and full-time homeschooler for her six children. She did marry young, although my parents convinced her to wait until she was twenty-one and nearly done with her undergraduate work. She went on to work in communications, complete graduate studies, work in epidemiological research, and collaborate on published papers.

My brother remains in Chicago, but he traded in the near-suburbia of our youth to live in a glass-walled high-rise overlooking the lake. He is a successful software developer, so passionate that even his free time is spent coding and sharing his work in open-source forums. He continues to play soccer and lead his adult league team, and despite my mother's pleading after each ankle injury and knee surgery, he has no plans as of yet to give it up.

I have lived on the East Coast and in the Midwest, in big cities, and now in another country within a semirural community. I have climbed mountains and hiked through Antarctica, jumped out of planes, and run half and full marathons. I put travel, graduate school, and career before parenthood, and now I'm an older mom with one child.

As when we were children, my siblings and I are very different as adults, but we are all productive and resilient. Most importantly, though, we have a great relationship with our parents and with each other.

When I was growing up, I watched how my mom parented my sister, brother, and me. I watched how she responded to each of us and to our individual interests, personalities, and needs. She knew how to appeal to our unspoken natures to get the best results with seemingly the least friction. It felt like she was raising each of us in a different way, yet it did not seem forced. It seemed natural. As a result of the parenting decisions made, each of us thrived in our own unique ways.

Perhaps guided by a fear of the future, some of my peers' parents followed an approach bordering on "helicopter" parenting. They seemed almost to be depending on their children's success as their own ticket to a new reality. These parents seemed ambitious, demanding, and driven. And it did not always work out as planned. I knew kids who responded to this pressure by rebelling and, to put it mildly, moving in directions their parents could not have anticipated. With less stress all around, my siblings and I were able to chart our individual paths and find happiness and success on our own terms.

My goal in writing this book is simple: I know my mom's organic parenting style works because I have lived it. As I continue on this grand parenting adventure with my own daughter, Lena, it is my intention to mimic those guiding principles my mom laid out. In the pages that follow, we share with you what we've learned along the way.

CITIZENS OF THE WORLD

Some ideas can best be shared through stories, which resonate differently for different people. It is my hope that the vignettes shared are entertaining, informational, and helpful to parents in the trenches.

Many years ago, when Kara's sister asked me for tips on child rearing, my rather offhanded reply was, "Raise children with whom you can live." At the time, I wondered if that was the response Nora expected. In retrospect, I think she was looking to me for some kind of magical parenting formula. The truth is, it doesn't exist.

When I was attending the University of Illinois as an undergrad, a social science professor told our class, "Your children will be children of the world." Say what? Although not fully understanding the implications, I internalized this statement as one more life task to complete without any explanation as to how. I filed the thought away in the "must plan to learn more" category.

Later, when I was married and planning for my first child, the professor's admonition came to mind. How was this citizen of the world business to take place? As a child of the Great Migration, I wasn't sure, but I committed to finding a way to raise a world-class child.

When Kara's sister was a toddler, my plan was to go back to school for a graduate degree. In my youthful mind, I assumed that I could rely on my mother to be a major parenting presence throughout those years. From my perspective at the time, my mom had done a good job of raising five successful and responsible children—and she'd done it while working the eleven-to-seven shift as an OB/GYN nurse. She taught us how to maintain the house while she was away. We learned how to look out for each other and how to rotate the daily chores, which included cooking, cleaning, washing, and ironing clothes. The house was clean and well organized. We were happy kids who did well in school.

Within two years of my marriage, I found myself spending more time at Mom's house than at my own. My beautiful and youthful-looking mother became a grandma when my first daughter was born, but she certainly didn't look like anybody's grandmother. She could have passed for a not-very-much-older sister. So, Mom became "Mama" and my daughter called me Connie. At one point, a playmate who wouldn't dare call her own parents by their first names, remarked alarmingly, "You mean you call your mother 'Connie'?"

Needless to say, life can be unpredictable. My plan fell through when Mom, after more than two decades juggling the night shift with being a single parent as well as active in our community, suddenly and unexpectedly was struck with a life-threatening illness. It was then that I really understood that being Mama to my child was my responsibility.

Before Mom passed away many years later, she shared with me that she had been determined to raise her children in a way that was different

18 · RAISING GRITTY KIDS

from the way she was brought up. In a sense, when the ball was in my court, it became my turn to figure out how best to get the parenting job done. These were the circumstances that inspired some deep thinking around what kind of parent I wanted to be.

I liked the idea of raising my children to be citizens of the world, to thrive in dynamic environments, and to find creative ways to contribute to their communities. One element of my strategy was to give my children gender-neutral toys, which meant dolls ("action figures," according to my son) as well as trucks and construction sets, with the idea that they would choose what they liked best.

I provided each of the three children with opportunities to learn foreign languages like Russian, Japanese, German, French, and Spanish, as well as music, the universal language. I looked for the best educational and extracurricular programs: Montessori, Suzuki, integrated public schools, summer camps, and activities where they could learn new skills and be exposed to diverse perspectives. Their horizons were further broadened through travel with family and friends.

We made use of those learning spaces in the city that at one time were not accessible to all: Chicago's wonderful museums, including the Art Institute, the Adler Planetarium, the Museum of Science and Industry, and the Field Museum. Regular trips to the library, to borrow books and attend workshops, became a significant part of my parenting strategy.

Looking back, I see how those early experiences in parenthood and my professor's admonition planted a seed that grew into this organic parenting style. Over time, I learned that it's okay to step outside of your community. It's okay not to keep doing whatever your family has done in the past. It's okay to try different schools, programs, and extracurricular activities for your children in order to find what will work best for them.

INTRODUCTION · 19

Take one day at a time, adapt as you go, look around and make use of things you have at hand.

I spent more than twenty years as an advocate for exceptional children with a range of socioemotional needs. This organic method proved highly successful. I would meet with the students, talk with their parents, ask about their grandparents, and really get to know each child so I could tailor an approach for working with him or her. I coached the parents of these students and encouraged them to trust themselves and to be their child's advocate, knowing the rest would fall into place.

Someone recently asked me, "Do you really want to call this organic parenting?" For now, it's the best way to describe this process. I have seen that organic parenting works—not only in my family but in other families as well. A lot of this is common sense, but important nuances can sometimes be overlooked. Having a framework can help. Rather than a one-size-fits-all approach, organic parenting provides a way for parents to adapt to each child's unique needs and interests.

HOW TO APPROACH THIS BOOK

We view this book as a conversation starter, not the final word on parenting. Writing it certainly generated a lot of conversation between my mom and me! We hope you will actively engage with these ideas, try them on for size, keep the ones you like, and put aside the ones that do not apply. Talk to the people who matter most in your life about the things you read here—friends, family, partners, teachers, spiritual guides, anyone who might shape your thinking on the grand exercise that is parenting.

Using this method leads to a personalized approach tailored for both parent and child. For me in particular, I have used my mom's example as a jumping-off point, but my parenting choices have been a little different from hers. What we have in common, though, is the way in which we think about parenting. By capturing both of our voices, we hope to illustrate the framework in action. There really is no right or wrong way to approach this book. First and foremost, it is a tool, and we hope you will use it as such.

Please note, this is not a book on the definitive way to raise a Noble Laureate or the next tech wunderkind. Our primary focus is on helping you raise decent, productive, ethical human beings in the least stressful way possible. To be perfectly honest, we are partly writing this book out of self-interest. We want to live in a world filled with well-balanced, moral, compassionate people. And it all starts with good parenting. So, thank you, parents, for picking up this book and hearing us out.

As one shepherds these precious little ones through life's early challenges, it is valuable to have some sense of the terrain they may have to traverse. No one gets it right 100 percent of the time, or even 100 percent right most of the time. But the process of thinking about the current landscape and how it may look in the future helps to lay the foundation. To that end, we begin our exploration of this organic parenting framework by looking out across the landscape.

"Where love is deep, much can be accomplished."

—Shinichi Suzuki

CHAPTER 1

Know the Landscape

"It is not the most intellectual of the species that survives; it is not the strongest that survives; but the species that survives is the one that is able best to adapt and adjust to the changing environment in which it finds itself."[3]

All over the internet, this quote is attributed to Charles Darwin's *On the Origin of Species*. The great irony, of course, is that these are not Darwin's words.

This quote apparently originated in an article by Leon Megginson, a professor of marketing and management at Louisiana State University in the 1960s and '70s. One of Megginson's former students said that a valuable lesson he learned from his instructor was that Darwin did not actually say that only the strong survive; rather, "What he said was that those who survive are the ones who most accurately perceive their environment and successfully adapt to it."[4]

For the purposes of our discussion of raising resilient children, what Darwin actually said is even more appropriate than the misquote. Case in point: the crocodile.

The crocodilian family has been around a long time, nearly 240 million years. Modern crocodiles are descended from prehistoric ancestors who survived two mass extinctions, one that killed the dinosaurs and another that wiped out large swaths of marine and other aquatic life.

Scientists are still learning why crocodiles have proven so resilient, given that other reptiles, such as turtles, have not fared as well through history. Researchers from the University of Bath's Milner Centre for Evolution recently weighed in, specifically considering how crocodiles have performed in periods of climate change. As part of the study, these scientists compared crocodiles' nesting habits with those of turtles.

What they found is instructive for us human parents. Year after year, many turtles return to the same nesting grounds to lay their eggs, regardless of the local environmental conditions and how they may have changed over the previous year. Mother turtles drop off their eggs in the sand and leave them to hatch alone and fend for themselves. Turtles, it seems, have embraced a rather hands-off parenting approach.

Crocodiles, on the other hand, carefully search out the nesting sites that are best for their offspring. If the environment in previously used sites is no longer suitable, crocodiles look elsewhere. They bury their eggs in rotting vegetation or earth, which protects the embryos from temperature fluctuation. The females tend to stay near the nest through the incubation period. And when the hatchlings begin to emerge, the mama crocodile returns to the nest to free her babies, carrying them in her mouth down to the water, where the new family will stay together, sometimes for months. Compared with turtles, crocodiles take a more hands-on approach, and as a result, their young have an easier time thriving amid changing conditions.

As inhabitants of the same planet—with its climate change, social and political shifts, and other changing conditions—humans can learn from the crocodile's example. Paying attention to the landscape and adapting as necessary based on what one sees (and foresees) can reap lifelong benefits for one's children.

Knowing the landscape serves a dual purpose. Primarily, understanding the terrain enables parents to chart the most positive path for the growth and development of their children. Secondarily, knowing the landscape gives parents an opportunity, through their parenting choices, to proactively shape the future environment their children will inherit. Both are crucial for raising gritty kids.

In this chapter, we will discuss the ways the social, cultural, and familial landscape has shifted from generation to generation, present a framework for thinking about and responding to the present and future landscape as it relates to your child, and provide tools to help you raise resilient children who thrive no matter what the future holds.

LEARN FROM THE PAST

Anyone looking back on 2020 is fully aware of the shifting nature of the landscape. One cannot escape it. The COVID-19 pandemic and its economic fallout have only added to the uncertainty around mismatched salaries and cost of living, rising home prices, and difficulty becoming anchored in a community.

Although the current upheavals may feel unprecedented, the reality is that times of great disruption come with near-cyclic regularity. Not to understate the gravity of our current times, but perspective is important. The specific sources of change may vary, but every generation has had its own uncertainties and its unique apprehension-and-anxiety track running in the background of everyday life.

During the 1950s, for example, with the backdrop of the Cold War, nuclear threat, and Communism, apprehensions for many were more geopolitical than financial. During the 1970s and '80s, anxieties centered on hyperinflation, AIDS, and a perception of increasing crime rates across the United States. Today, we have staggering wealth inequality, a social justice reckoning, and the impending threat of ever-more-extreme climate events with which to wrestle.

Generations of Americans have witnessed shifts in family composition, the entrance of more women into the workforce, and growing diversity across the land. Each shift has brought new challenges—and possibilities—for parents helping their children navigate the world around them.

As a parent, it can be helpful to learn from past generations and to understand that things have always been shifting and will continue to do so. Gaining this insight can inform your decisions and increase your confidence that you indeed have everything it takes to make the best choices given your current landscape and your child.

The best place to start with understanding the landscape you find yourself in is in your own backyard. The environment in which my mom grew up was vastly different from the one

26 · RAISING GRITTY KIDS

in which I was raised. Our extended family's geographical location, the social and political climate, the available activities and resources, and more changed significantly over the course of a few decades. Likewise, the environment in which I am raising my daughter differs from both my mom's and my own experiences. The parenting choices that my grandmother made were appropriate then. The same goes for my mom and her choices. It is important to note that the choices that are more readily available to me with my daughter would not have been possible or feasible in my grandmother's day.

Much of my mom's organic parenting style springs from looking at the past landscapes in general and in our family history specifically, considering the parenting techniques various ones have used, borrowing what makes sense, and finding new strategies when the past ones are no longer applicable.

FAMILY LANDSCAPES

My younger years were spent in the South. Dad worked and Mom stayed at home when my siblings and I were young. We had lots of extended family nearby. My mother filled her days with sewing and cooking lessons. At bedtime she read to us from her favorite books of poetry and collections of short stories. Looking back, it is likely that from these readings we learned cultural values. Mom's selections tended to emphasize the importance of love—for example, in Shakespeare's "Sonnet 116" or the "Gift of the Magi" by O. Henry. Characteristic of the times, she didn't talk to us directly about these things. There was no moralizing or pointing out life lessons. That came with regular church attendance. My siblings and I created our own entertainment. We didn't visit museums or libraries. At that time, sports training was virtually unheard of and formal music lessons were rare.

Kara's landscape was quite different. By the time she was born, our family had settled in the North, and fundamental sociocultural features of the country were in a state of flux. For example, I don't think that Kara or her peers understood in the deep way I did the ramifications, for some people, of the Mason-Dixon Line, which divided the North and the South.

Extended family lived much farther away, but opportunities for sports training like gymnastics and soccer or music lessons were easily accessible. Kara attended schools with diverse ethnic demographics, and we lived near excellent, easily accessible museums.

In raising Kara and her siblings, about 25 percent of my challenge was how to relate to their experience when it had not been my own. This might sound like a lot, but it was actually more fun than meets the eye.

Here's an example: the library. When I was a child, we did not visit the library, but it became a favorite spot for Kara, and I worked to include her interest into our weekly schedule.

When not quite four years old, Kara asked the local librarian about checking out some books. The thoughtful lady carefully explained that she needed a library card, but couldn't get one until she could sign her name. "Can you sign your name, sweetie?" she asked, smiling at the articulate little girl.

Kara was disappointed and surprisingly resolute. After returning home, she secretly practiced writing her name over and over again for several days. So, when the time came for the next visit to the library, she was ready. At the check-out desk, she announced to the librarian, "I can sign my name. Can I get a library card now?" Both surprised and charmed, the librarian consented, and Kara got her card.

Learning new things and meeting new people can be a positive adventure for both parent and child.

UNDERSTAND THE PRESENT, SHAPE THE FUTURE

Here is a mantra for today's parents: remember the crocodile. As explained earlier, this resilient reptile carefully evaluates its environment and makes decisions that give its offspring the best chance of thriving—an excellent model of knowing the current landscape while keeping an eye on the future and making parenting decisions accordingly.

As a parent, you stand in your present landscape, which likely includes a mix of financial, environmental, social, and, to some extent, geopolitical realities you will want to consider to best help your child navigate the future. Fully recognizing that no one of us has the benefit of a crystal ball, I offer a couple high-level questions to get started: Twenty years from now, will concerns be primarily financial or social? Or will climate change become the biggest source of apprehension?

My husband and I are analytical by nature. Some of our earliest dates involved attending science lectures and staying afterward to pepper the featured speakers with in-depth questions. Early in our marriage, we pondered the morality and reasonableness of having children today in the face of seemingly inevitable climate change. It was our hope that the world would come together to make the necessary changes to shore up the environment for future generations.

When at last we took the plunge into parenthood, I spent time on my own contemplating what the world might look like for our daughter. As Lena grows, the landscape seems to be shifting ever more rapidly. I regularly peer out into the world and consider how what I see will affect my daughter's future. Here is just a smattering of the specific questions I find myself turning over in my mind:

- How will climate change shape Lena's life as an adult? What kinds of environments will people live in? Will they still live in cities? What will home and community look like and mean to people?
- What is the future of higher education? Even before COVID-19, online education was becoming more widely accepted. As the trend accelerates, what are the chances that Lena will have a traditional on-campus experience similar to the formative time I spent at Harvard and later Wharton?
- What is the future of work? What skills and ways of thinking will be valued in twenty years? With the rise of automation and artificial intelligence, will there come a time when people do not work at all? And if that happens, how will humans spend their days?

Underpinning all of these considerations is one foundational concern: what I can do right now to help my daughter to be resilient long into the future. Thinking through what may lie ahead has had a tangible impact on the choices I make today. For example, I believe higher education will look vastly different by the time Lena is ready to attend, and that has changed the way I am saving for college. As I think about the future of work, my opinions on various extracurricular programs have subtly shifted, and I now see language acquisition as being of prime importance.

When I was growing up, my mom emphasized long-term thinking and the accrued benefit from an incremental investment in developing skills and discipline. She encouraged us to explore the things we enjoyed, but there was also a practical side to her guidance. Passion projects were well and good, but she was always concerned with how we would make a living and thrive.

Just as I am doing today, my mom looked out on the landscape, understood that things were changing, and considered how best to position her kids for what was coming. Having us involved in music, science, and sports programs required no little sacrifice on her part. Not every parent makes that choice, but Mom believed these training grounds were necessary to prepare us for what was coming next.

My mom worked long days in demanding classroom environments and then shepherded one or more of us to and from sports practice or music lessons or extracurricular academic activities. During the summer, she shuttled us to educational camps and programs, sometimes driving an hour-plus each way for classes that started at seven thirty in the morning. Mom did not look at this as a sacrifice. She saw it as an opportunity. In her view, we lived in Chicago, with its vibrant cultural offerings, a veritable smorgasbord, and as a parent, it was her responsibility to share with us the possibilities of this larger world.

Through a math and science teachers' program at the Illinois Institute of Technology, my siblings and I had early exposure to computers. My dad is an electrical engineer, and our family always had the latest technology and gadgets. We had a personal computer long before most people in our community, and we lugged that thirty-pound IBM 5155 "portable" PC to the math and science lab at school so other children could tinker with it. Mom knew computers were going to be a huge part of the future and she wanted other children, not just her own, to have access to this technology. In doing so, she exposed all of us to this wave of the future, piquing our curiosity and shifting the range of possibility for the larger community of children in her orbit.

KNOW THE LANDSCAPE · 31

Mom's actions point to a key truth. You are not parenting in a fixed, unchanging environment. There are always options. If you look out and do not like what you see, you can indeed shape the future landscape for your children with a bit of creative thinking and the will to do things in a different way.

People questioned various of my mom's parenting choices, not least of which was the decision to have each of us commute to schools outside our community. My brother and I spent hours each day getting to and from our elementary schools. Some in our extended family felt that in pursuing this option, our mom unnecessarily put us in harm's way by sending us into potentially hostile terrain on school buses that got into occasional fender-benders.

In her defense, our mom was playing the long game. She wanted us to become children of the world. She wanted our minds and hearts to be open to people of various ethnicities and socioeconomic backgrounds. Above all, she wanted us to receive the best education possible.

As a result of these early choices, my siblings and I all had exposure to a wide array of cultures, and we have formed life-long friendships with all kinds of interesting people. No doubt, the ease I feel meeting new people and learning about new places has made it that much easier to navigate life's challenges and embrace the many "adventures" that have presented themselves along the way. Because of my exposure to unfamiliar situations at a young age, it felt okay for me to set out in different directions beyond what otherwise might have been proscribed for a little girl growing up on Chicago's South Side.

"The child is capable of developing and giving us tangible proof

of the possibility of a better humanity...The child is both a hope and a promise for mankind."

—MARIA MONTESSORI, *EDUCATION AND PEACE*

In an interview with Ezra Klein of *Vox*, world-renowned Harvard economist Raj Chetty talked about social mobility between generations and how the role of exposure to a variety of people and experiences in childhood can significantly impact one's prospects. Chetty says, "One of the strongest patterns that emerges in all of these studies is that what you're exposed to as a child—in terms of career pathways, crime, marriage, etc.—impacts how you grow up." He gives the example of a study of inventors that showed that if women grow up in an area where there are more female inventors, they are more likely to become inventors themselves. However, if there are more male inventors in that area, it has no impact on the girls. "These patterns are very specific, and they reflect the fact that children absorb what's in their family and what's in their surroundings."[5]

The path a person ultimately takes reflects their horizon of possibility. As Klein notes, "Not everything is about material benefits, not everything is about direct chances."[6] Simply seeing that something is within the realm of the possible can be enough to nudge your child in a direction that may not have been open to you. My mom understood this innately, and it shaped her ongoing analysis of the trade-offs she made in time, money, and ease. It was not always the comfortable path, but it was the one that she believed would best serve us throughout life.

Looking out across one's landscape and seeing what's possible is important in shaping outcomes for children. Parents should try always to keep in mind what is in a child's view of what is possible. This applies equally for the negative as well as the positive. If for no other reason than that it will broaden his or her horizon of possibility, exposure to diversity of all types can be valuable in building your child's resiliency.

THINKING ABOUT THE LANDSCAPE

We have already covered a number of directions in which you could take your explorations of the landscape. For those looking for another way to think through the larger forces at work on a local and societal level, the ecological systems theory of Urie Bronfenbrenner may be useful.

Trained as a developmental psychologist, Bronfenbrenner was instrumental in helping to craft early education programs in the United States. One idea he shared was that children developed into successful adults through sustained, positive interaction with their parents and surrounded by supportive society. Ecological systems theory formalized this idea. His model maps out ever-widening spheres of influence, starting with the child in the middle and working out to the society at large. From a policy perspective, the ecological systems theory may have its complications, but as a way to organize one's thinking about the landscape, it can be useful.

Our organic parenting framework corresponds somewhat to Bronfenbrenner's focus on the individual child as the center of the model. However, we take a deeper dive to consider how your child's unique mental, physical, emotional, social, and ethical/spiritual makeup can be encouraged and developed through childhood and into early adulthood.

34 · RAISING GRITTY KIDS

Much like our notion of knowing the landscape, Bronfenbrenner suggests conceptualizing the interactions between the social groups in which your family lives and operates—for example, between the family and school, between peers and the child, or between church and family. It can be useful to consider these, especially where priorities and values may be in conflict, in order to address or minimize the number of mixed messages being sent to the child.

Another aspect to consider is whether the relative importance of any of these areas is shifting for your family and for the society at large. Bronfenbrenner emphasized that the relationships between the social groups themselves are dynamic. In other words, the landscape can be shaped and changed for the better as the parent sees a need to do so.

Finally, who and what comprise these immediate communities shape the child's horizon of possibility. Take a quick inventory of what your child might be observing that could be shaping thoughts about the world. Bronfenbrenner, like Chetty, recommends exposure to diverse ethnic, social, religious, and other background factors to enhance the child's development on the journey to self-sufficiency.

Theoretical systems are important especially for policymakers, but as a parent in the trenches sometimes facing stressful situations and decisions, I have found it especially helpful to have a set of real-life parenting strategies to apply here and now. Building on the idea that one size does not fit all, our aim in this book is to share a jumping-off point for parents to actualize the parenting style that works best for them and their child.

SHIFTING PARENTING ADVICE

As a young adult, one persistent worry I had about having children one day was that somehow, I would not be up to the task. Although my mom never said as much, I had the definite sense growing up that there was an overarching philosophy guiding her parenting decisions. As I tried to envision myself in the role of "Mama," comparisons to my mom snuck in at every turn. Here she was, an expert, having worked with thousands of children over the years, with a graduate degree in education and childhood psychology. The bar was high, frighteningly high, and I feared I would be a failure at parenting.

I do not think my mom really knew what a giant shadow she cast over this aspect of my life until years later. What finally had me move past my fears was an acknowledgment that parenting would be an adventure, the greatest of my life, and that as long I led with my heart, sought out advice from those I trusted, and put my faith in my ability to learn and grow and improve, I would figure it all out.

Another thing that helped was finally accepting that although this was a huge decision in the context of my life, I also needed to take a broader perspective. As a species, humans are pretty tough. People have been having babies for millennia, making good and bad parenting decisions, listening to the sometimes hilariously wacky advice of experts, fighting, crying, and loving their children with all they've got. One has only to look at how parenting advice has shifted over time to understand that most of us are doing the best we can with what we know at any given point in time.

If you have ever felt the doubts creep in, or the anxiety from

36 · RAISING GRITTY KIDS

wondering if maybe you are doing it all wrong, I offer some examples from the past to help assuage your fears. Remember that these were the conditions your great-grandparents and grandparents may have experienced, and they lived to tell the tale. For example, *A Handbook of Obstetric Nursing*, published in 1895, suggests that to hold a baby any more than to feed and clean it will "foolishly spoil" the child, laying the groundwork for its future as "a little tyrant." Better to "train" the baby to be "contented and happy as it lies in its crib," alone for hours at a stretch.[7]

The 1928 book *Psychological Care of Infant and Child* offers advice favoring a similarly detached, hands-off approach:

> Never hug and kiss them or let them sit on your lap. Shake hands with them in the morning, give them a pat on the head if they've made an extraordinarily good job of a difficult path.[8]

Even Eleanor Roosevelt had some parenting techniques that many people would shake their heads at today:

> I had a curious arrangement out of one of my back windows for airing the children, kind of a box with wire on the sides and top. Anna was put out there for her morning nap. On several occasions, she wept loudly. Finally, one of my neighbors called up and said I was treating my children inhumanely and that she would report me to the SPCC if I did not take her in at once. This was a shock for me for I thought I was being a most modern mother. I knew fresh air is necessary, but I learned later that the sun is more important than the air. I had left her on the shady side of the house.[9]

After World War II, a shift started, which called into question the value of such disengaged methods. With the introduction of Dr. Benjamin Spock's *Common Sense Book of Baby and Child Care*, a more responsive style was born. By the 1980s, the pendulum had swung full stop when Dr. William Sears and his wife, Martha, laid the foundation for what would later be termed "attachment parenting." One of the defining features of this style is that it advocates for keeping the child in close proximity at all times, literally attached in a sling for as many hours during the day as possible when the child is an infant.

While true attachment parenting and immersion mothering can be incredibly draining and exhausting, particularly for mothers who are juggling baby care with work, current research does show advantages to developing a love-forward, secure attachment with a child when he is young. Developmental psychologist Alan Sroufe has gone as far as saying, "Nothing is more important than the attachment relationship." After nearly forty years studying the role that attachment style plays in children's future outcomes, Sroufe determined,

> One of the most important (and paradoxical) findings was that a secure attachment early in life led to greater independence later, whereas an insecure attachment led children to be more dependent later in life.[10]

If your aim is to foster independence and autonomy in your children, both of which are essential components of resilience, the best indications are that developing a secure attachment will pay dividends. The long list of benefits that Dr. Sroufe found includes better emotional regulation, higher self-esteem, and better coping under stress—all important in raising children who can thrive amidst the changes that might be coming.

Hopefully, this sampling of past and present advice has convinced you that no one absolutely knows what is best. Researchers learn, get a sense of what actually works, and shift their recommendations. At the end of the day, we are all still learning. Seeing the variation in these styles should give you license not to stress over your own parenting decisions. If you can look at current research, take what works for you in your current situation, and not sweat the rest too much, your child and your sanity will thank you. As Dr. Spock notably said, "Trust yourself. You know more than you think you do."[11]

KNOW THE LANDSCAPE TOOL KIT

Here are a few suggestions for starting an exploration of your landscape—past, present, and future—as well as the parenting choices you want to make based on what you see.

THINK AND DISCUSS

Knowing the landscape starts with thinking about what you see. For a fun flashback, check out Bronfenbrenner's talk from 1976 entitled "The American Family. Who Cares?" It is widely available online and instructive both in terms of thinking about landscape as well as providing perspective on how little has changed in the decades since. If your child is old enough, engage her in conversation about how she sees her landscape and how it appears—at school, in peer groups, and in other social outlets.

SHARE YOUR FAMILY HISTORY

Storytelling is an important way to explore the past landscape, but it can be difficult to make time to share family history. Your children (and their children) can benefit from learning about the life experiences of prior generations.

Take time to talk to your children about your experiences growing up. If you are so inclined, put pen to paper and record thoughts for your children to read as they get older. Encourage them to ask questions. Whenever convenient, use pictures and maps in the process of telling your family history. Using visual methods to ground your stories will make them all the more resonant for your child, particularly if she is more visual by nature.

In this sidebar, my mom talks about the importance of family history and shares a story written by her mom, my grandmother.

• •

FAMILY HISTORY

It's been nearly a decade since Stephen Hawking asked the question, "Are we losing our moorings?" Long before COVID-19, he asked humankind to think critically about our future as a species. "In a world that is in chaos politically, socially, and environmentally, how can the human race sustain another hundred years? I don't know the answer. That is why I asked the question: to get people to think."[12]

In previous eras, a child's future was pretty much determined. He was likely to remain in the town, village, or neighborhood in which he was born. His livelihood would be derived in the same way as his father's: baker, soldier, farmer, shopkeeper, autoworker, steelworker, minister, doctor, lawyer, aristocrat, gentleman, lady, servant, or slave. That's no longer the case. We live in a new place and time, and many still believe in the American Dream. So, how do you best prepare your child for the future, given the shifting nature of the present?

In general, start by asking questions. Adopting a learn-as-you-go mindset can help you avoid panic. As you uncover answers, you can take constructive steps to guide your child in the direction that will be most helpful. That is part of the essence of organic parenting.

You can also look to nature. Teach your children how to share the earth with other living things. Show them how to observe by visiting a zoo, ranch, farm—even your own backyard.

You can start a garden, which can be exciting and fun as the child gets a chance to see plants evolve from seedlings. It is well established that gardening has numerous benefits, from observing the wonders of nature, to encouraging healthy eating habits, to getting more physical exercise.

Most importantly, learn and share your family history. The query of nineteenth-century artist Paul Gauguin pertains even today. He asked, "D'où venons nous? Que sommes nous? Où allons nous?" (From where do we come? What are we? Where are we going?) Similarly, another popular saying advises that if you don't know from whence you came, you won't know where you're going. One more simply states that it's important to know family history so we don't repeat mistakes.

If you want to help your child become more grounded, one way is to share both maternal and paternal family history, if possible. At times, these histories can be complicated. However, an authentic narrative contributes to a sense of balance.

The story that follows comes from a small book of family stories written

KNOW THE LANDSCAPE · 41

by my mother.[13] "The Out House" is her recollection of the landscape as a five-year-old growing up on Florida's Gulf Coast. Imagine Kara's surprise at first learning that people back then didn't have indoor plumbing! Use this piece as inspiration for recording your own stories for your children and future generations.

The Out House

You could tell how well off a family was by looking at the "out-house" in back of their home. How well -built it was; how clean it was. At our home, house cleaning extended all the way to the outhouse or as mama called it, "the lavatory." She'd go out with a bucket of sudsy water that smelled of disinfectant. Then she'd use the special broom that she kept in the tidy little 'house.' Scrubbing and rinsing included the seats as well as the floor. Our privy had an adult seat and child's seat built-in with a huge, barrel-sized bucket set underneath each. The man who drove the doo-doo truck would stop at each house and he and his assistant would dump the contents of these containers into the massive one on the back of his truck. When the men replaced the toilet cans, they always dusted a white powdery substance labeled "LIME" generously in and around the cans.

Even the walls were liberally doused. The door was propped open so that the sun and warm tropical breezes could complete the cleansing process. Then mama would bring out the big Sears and Roebuck catalog or a Montgomery Ward catalog and set it beside the adult seat. She set the smaller McClellan's catalog beside the child's seat. All's finished now, except that the odor from the big truck lingered on for awhile.

I was always afraid to go into the church outhouse because the church was located down a little path in the woods, and there would be spiders and wasp nests. The chameleons, which could stay very still, and then jump suddenly, were not easily recognizable because they could change their color to match wood or leaves or tree bark or whatever.

Great Auntie lived eight miles in the country, but she and Great Uncle had a big family of adult children living on the farm. There were lots of cousins, cows, horses and chickens, turkeys, ducks and guineas; even two dogs and a cat. I loved it out there because there were all kinds of fruit trees: peach, plum, orange and grapefruit, even tangerine trees.

There was a big playhouse in the side yard for the children (unless, of course, you were very tall for your age). Their outhouse was away down a swept path and had a 'croaker' sack covering for the door.

Our one-room school outhouse was for the boys and girls to share. Our teacher would let the girls out first "for relief." Then when girls were back inside and seated, the boys were allowed to go out. There were six seats and a tall wood fence stood in front. The outhouse was always nice and clean. The Sears and Roebuck catalog was always kind of dog-eared. This from so many little hands checking out the toys and school supplies, et cetera.

. . . .

CONSIDER MENTAL MODELS

The blog *Farnam Street* discusses the mental models through which people make sense of their world and the environment.[14] Out of the top one hundred mental models, several are especially relevant to parenting in general and this idea of knowing your landscape in particular.

Probabilistic Thinking

Probabilistic thinking involves trying to estimate the likelihood of any specific outcome coming to pass. This mental model can help reduce anxiety around uncertainty. For exam-

KNOW THE LANDSCAPE · 43

ple, to know that something might happen, though it is highly unlikely, could be reassuring. However, if something is highly likely to happen, it might be a good idea to plan ahead.

Surveying the landscape in the context of parenting is fundamentally an exercise in probabilistic thinking. You peer out over the range of outcomes and course correct your actions based on which you think are most likely to occur. Earlier, I gave the example of how I believe strongly that the college experience will come to be very different from what it once was. As a result, I've changed my behavior in how I'm saving for Lena's future, acknowledging that it very well may not include going to university and living on campus for the duration.

The Red Queen Effect

This model is derived from Lewis Carroll's *Through the Looking Glass*, where Alice, of Wonderland fame, finds herself once again navigating a world of illusion. The Red Queen explains the nature of Looking-Glass Land, telling Alice, "Now, *here*, you see, it takes all the running you can do, to keep in the same place."[15]

The idea is that when one species evolves an advantageous adaptation, the competing species must respond in kind or fall behind and ultimately fail. One must keep improving to get ahead.

This is important as you look out across your landscape. If you understand things are changing, that some people are developing an advantage in some sphere, and you pretend it's not happening, you (and your children) will likely fall behind.

44 · RAISING GRITTY KIDS

When we were growing up, my mother understood that the internet and computer technologies would be society-changing forces. Although she claims to be a neo-Luddite herself, she encouraged us to embrace these changes and learn all we could so that we would be more competitive in the future.

Compounding

Compounding is the process by which we add interest to our initial investment, creating an exponential effect rather than a linear one. Money in a savings account compounds, albeit very slowly these days. Investments in learning and in building relationships compound as well. Even ten minutes of quality time spent with your child each day can pay off in relationship dividends and trust far into the future.

My mom understood the power of compounding very well when it came to honing our cognitive acuity and critical thinking skills, both of which are important for long-term resiliency. She snuck in little bits of mental math and problem-solving in our everyday lives from the time my siblings and I were old enough to count and have conversations. These mini problem-solving sessions never felt arduous because they were fun and fast. Over time, without us realizing it, the problems grew more complicated and our ability to collaborate and think through complex questions in our heads and on the fly was well established. Mom invested in our learning early and consistently, which required an investment of her focus and time, and it has paid off.

We invite you to read about these mental models and more at https://fs.blog/mental-models/. You can use these as tools to think through Bronfenbrenner's theory, as discussed earlier. Have some fun with it. For example, using these models, consider the following questions:

- What is the landscape like today? What are the largest social and technological forces impacting our lives right now? What trends are gaining traction? Which ones might fundamentally change the ways in which we live today?
- What changes do you think are relevant? Which ones do you have control over? How can you best position your family to thrive in the face of these changes?
- Are there any elements that are distractions or detours from moving forward? How can you mitigate their impact?

REMEMBER THE CROCODILE

As a parent, you want what is best for your child. Setting him up for future success starts with thinking about the landscape, considering what it might look like, and then making choices to position your child as best you can.

Some skills cannot be acquired overnight. Developing them requires an investment of time, time that cannot be recovered once it is lost. If you feel like a skill or trait is going to be important in the future, start working on it when your child is young, rather than trying to rush things later.

This chapter has been filled with questions, probably more than anywhere else in this book. This is by design. Knowing your landscape is the springboard from which the rest of your parenting efforts take off. Take time to think through the questions posed and consider the areas where your priorities may have changed.

46 · RAISING GRITTY KIDS

If nothing else, we know this: change is always happening, and landscapes are always shifting. So, embrace your inner crocodile and your child will thrive.

In the next chapter, we consider knowing your child, the second principle of our parenting framework.

CHAPTER 2

Know Your Child

"One test of the correctness of educational procedure is the happiness of the child itself."

—MARIA MONTESSORI, *WHAT YOU
SHOULD KNOW ABOUT YOUR CHILD*

• •

SUPERGIRL

Many children go through a superhero stage. As daring seven- and eight-year-olds, my brother and I once donned make-believe capes created from discarded bed sheets and we prepared to "fly" from the roof of our grandparents' backyard storage building.

When Nora was about nine, she was certain that she could lift the rear end of the car. We had just seen *Superman*, and our little girl assumed she, too, had superpowers. Her dad and I watched incredulously as she walked to the back of the car while challenging us to "watch this." The tears came when the car wouldn't budge. Nora was deeply embarrassed. We had to assure her that it was okay and that we loved her.

Kara's superhero moment came when she was five years old.

"Mom, I think I broke my arm." To this day, I can still hear those words.

"Are you playing?" I asked from the kitchen, where I was preparing dinner. She said it again, calmly and matter-of-factly, "I think I broke my arm."

I didn't think it was possible since the footstool was less than twelve inches from the floor, which was covered with thick carpeting. However, Kara didn't usually play like that. Even though she wasn't crying, it sounded serious.

I left the lasagna and walked into the family room. She was lying on the floor next to the ottoman and sure enough, her arm was bent and twisted in a most unusual way. Some years later, Kara shared with me that she wasn't afraid until she saw the look on my face taking in the scene.

Not ten minutes earlier, Kara had been in the kitchen watching me prepare dinner. I had asked her to go to the family room so I could finish. She pouted her way to the other room and started twirling off the ottoman, pretending to be Supergirl, arms outstretched and ready to take flight. After a few successful fast-flying twirls, our quiet Saturday afternoon took a turn.

I called out to my husband. I think he heard the panic in my voice because he rushed into the room. He lifted Kara gently into his arms, careful not to disturb her right arm, which she said was beginning to shoot excruciating rays of pain. Dinner prep sat half done as we all rushed out the door for the short drive to our local emergency room.

When we arrived, we were ushered to an examination room. The nurse approached with shears to cut off Kara's blouse so as not to disturb the injury. Our little girl looked so small and vulnerable as we watched them wheel her away to the radiology department. The attending physician needed X-rays to assess the nature of the break, but even to the naked

50 · RAISING GRITTY KIDS

eye, it looked bad. That tiny arm was bent in such an odd way; it hurts me to this day to recall. The ER doctor determined that this was no ordinary break and decided to call a pediatric orthopedic surgeon from across town to come for a consultation.

When the surgeon arrived, he examined Kara, looked at the X-rays, and then pulled me aside to explain the seriousness of the injury and our options for setting Kara's arm. The strategy that would ultimately yield the best results involved nearly a month in traction. The doctor wasn't sure if this would work for Kara because it would require immobilizing her arm, and for all intents and purposes, keeping her anchored to the hospital bed in the same position for the duration. She was only five and it seemed a lot to ask.

"Let's talk to her about it," I said.

The doctor looked a little unsure, but he said okay and we both turned back to Kara. The doctor explained that she would have to stay in the hospital for three and a half weeks, with her arm suspended by wires and weights. He emphasized that in order for the healing process to work, she would not be able to move.

When he finished, I asked Kara, "Do you understand what the doctor is saying?"

Kara nodded, affirming that she understood and thought she could do it.

I stayed with Kara that first night to help with the adjustment. But after that, her father and I could only see her during regular visiting hours. This was Kara's first time away from home, and she spent long, lonely days with the television for company and braved nights punctuated with the blinking lights and strange beeps emanating from machines whirring all around.

KNOW YOUR CHILD · 51

Even though she was only five years old, I knew my daughter well enough to know that this would be okay. I knew that I could describe the situation, have a conversation about what would be required, and give her a choice in what happened next. This thought was consoling.

• •

About five years after I broke my arm, I had another freak accident. This time I was in phys-ed class, and we were running warm-up laps around the gym when I tripped and fell. I knew right away that something was seriously wrong.

As I had when I was five, I calmly stated my situation. This time, however, I was met with a very different reaction from the adult in charge.

When I said, "I think I broke my foot," the teacher became irritated and snapped back, "That's ridiculous. Keep running."

"No, really," I insisted. "I think I broke my foot."

At that point, the teacher's irritation morphed into downright anger, and he waved me away. I knew something was wrong and that something needed to be done because I couldn't put any weight on that foot. So, I hopped over to the wall and clinging to it the whole way, gingerly dragged myself to the office so I could get some help.

My mom came as fast as Chicago's midday traffic would allow. We headed straight to the hospital to get X-rays, and indeed, I had broken my foot. It is likely that the break had been exacerbated in my clumsy attempt to get to the office. I returned

52 · RAISING GRITTY KIDS

to school the next day wearing a fiberglass boot up to my knee and hobbling around on crutches.

In response to my injured status and my inability to participate, the gym teacher gave me a C for that quarter. For a regularly straight-A student, this was particularly disheartening. It felt like punishment because I had taken matters into my own hands when he would not listen. This was far from the last time I would stand up to an authority figure and pay the price. But I had the self-confidence, even then, to know what was the right course of action for me. And I was not afraid to advocate for myself.

I think the main difference between this situation and the one when I broke my arm was that this teacher did not really know me. He had hundreds of students and probably had not paid much attention to each of us outside of our ability to do pull-ups or play kickball.

The truth is, I had always participated in gym class. I had never faked an injury or illness or in any way tried to get out of an activity. Because the teacher did not notice or remember that, he did not trust me or my assessment. He did not know me well enough to know that I would not joke around about something like a broken foot. As a result, I did not receive the immediate care that I needed like I had when I broke my arm. Fun fact: my arm, which suffered a far worse break, healed perfectly, but my foot gives me problems to this day.

This compare-and-contrast of my childhood injuries illustrates the point of this chapter: to know what parenting decision is best in any given situation, you have to know your child. To this end, chapter 2 explores the importance of observing, conversing with, and responding to your child so that your parenting choices consider your child's particular personality and preferences. The chapter ends with a tool kit to help in your endeavor to know your child.

OBSERVE, ASK, AND LISTEN

In *The Absorbent Mind*, Maria Montessori says teachers "must have a kind of faith that the child will reveal himself through work."[16] This is equally applicable to parents: observe your child and let him reveal himself—his personality, interests, spiritual sensibility, responsiveness to correction, strengths, weaknesses, and more. Taking note of these things requires a certain level of stillness and a willingness to step back and simply watch.

As parents observe, they get to see where their child's interests are, how she responds to difficult tasks, what comes easy, where she might be struggling. Rather than immediately stepping in when a child falters, parents should stand by and see what the child does.

This is definitely an area where I struggle. As a working parent, I am trying to accomplish so many things, which has fueled my strivings for ultra-efficiency. Sometimes I find myself literally sitting on my hands to keep myself from reaching out to do things for my daughter—things that would take me two seconds to complete. Yet I understand that she needs to go through the process of doing it herself, of practicing to improve, and finally of feeling empowered by the accomplishment. It is difficult at times, but my commitment to seeing Lena develop her life skills tool kit is greater than the discomfort I sometimes feel when it is not the most efficient way to get things done.

54 · RAISING GRITTY KIDS

Observation is only one part of knowing your child. Unless parents ask questions and engage their child in conversation, they will not truly know what the child is thinking. Reading together and sharing family stories can come in handy here. As in knowing the landscape, stories provide opportunities for children to ask questions and share their perspective. Parents should encourage this kind of dialogue with their children from a young age in order to learn how the child thinks, processes information, and makes connections.

Many years after the incident when Nora tried to exercise her superpowers, she shared her thinking as a child. She told our mom that the fact that she had attended five different schools before the age of ten left her feeling a strong need to be powerful enough to control her world. Our mom didn't see that coming. From her perspective, those moves were made always in Nora's best interest.

Knowing the child is a constantly evolving activity because the child is constantly evolving herself as she experiences new environments, acquires skills, and gains confidence. Brain development happens so quickly in young children that it's often better to reserve judgment about "the way he is" or "what he likes." Even personality traits that seem fixed at one point can transform into something else in time. You just have to keep checking in to see how your little one's preferences are changing.

· ·

KNOWING INVOLVES LISTENING

Steve, a family friend, and I met at our state senator's office to discuss additional funding for a local academic program. While we waited for the senator, we chatted. Steve shared that he was puzzled and concerned about some unexpected attitudes his son was displaying.

Steve and his very successful wife were raised in a suburban community, pretty much lacking in diversity of any kind. Now living in the city, they had decided to use their privilege to make a different choice, to make sure their son had a broader experience. They transferred their son to a high school known for its multicultural emphasis that brought teens together from all corners of the state—rural, suburban, and urban. In the months since their son started classes, he had started saying some pretty ugly things.

As it turned out, Steve and his wife were deeply involved in their demanding careers and found little time to hear from their son about how the transition to the new school was going. Without talking to him, there was no way to know exactly what was happening.

My suggestion to Steve was to set aside an uninterrupted block of time to hear his son's perspective.

The next time I saw Steve, I asked him for an update. It seemed that his son was being teased by a group of "fun" guys at school. His son's demeanor said "jock" more than "serious student," and peers assumed the new kid on the block would join the group of popular party boys. In reality, he enjoyed his academic interests and preferred spending time at the library to hanging out in the game room. He had no idea why he had become a target for teasing when all he really wanted was to keep to himself. Perhaps the taunters were feeling rejected. Or they thought they could pressure him into joining them. Either way, Steve's son didn't have anyone to talk to about what was happening until his father opened up the conversation.

Steve shared with me, "We thought we'd done everything right, that we'd made all the right choices. How did we miss this?" They needed to hear their son's voice to understand what he was seeing. Then, they were able to address the issue together.

• •

ACTIVE LISTENING IN PARENTING

Some parenting philosophies follow a one-way model, directed primarily by the parent. The parent creates the rules, sets the boundaries, and makes the decisions, with little input from the child. This is known as an authoritarian style, which is high in demandingness (the tendency to demand responsible, mature behavior by the child) but low in responsiveness (the amount a parent responds to the child's needs). There is little focus on knowing the child with this style of parenting.

The authoritarian style is not to be confused with the authoritative style, which is characterized as high in both demandingness and responsiveness. Constructive responsiveness is rooted in knowing your child.

According to Dr. Judith Locke and colleagues, numerous studies have concluded that authoritative parenting is the most effective at improving children's well-being in areas such as self-esteem, self-reliance, having a sense of security, and popularity with peers.[17] In short, if parents can simultaneously expect mature behavior and respond to their child's needs, then they are more likely to raise resilient children.

What we are proposing is a bidirectional, responsive style in the spirit of authoritative parenting. Parents still set boundaries and expectations, but they also respond to the child: the

KNOW YOUR CHILD · 57

interests developing, the strengths and weaknesses exhibited, and so on. In a sense, this model emphasizes constant communication between the parent and child, with the responsibilities on the child growing ever greater over time.

To be responsive, parents must know their child. They must understand the child's needs and interests and then actively respond to them. In demanding responsible and mature behavior, parents are looking for areas of potential weakness where they can provide guidance and practice.

When my brother was around age eight, he developed an interest in playing soccer, but this was no ordinary interest. It was the start of a lifelong passion, one could even say obsession. David wanted to be captain of his team. He wanted to direct the movements of the other little kids as they mapped out the plays. And he wanted to wow opponents with his fancy footwork, agility, and speed.

Our mom did not know much about soccer at the time. But after doing some research, she found training camps focused on soccer, enrolled my brother in an advanced sports physics class so he could learn more about the on-field dynamics at play, and spent countless hours kicking the ball around with him at a playground near our house. She did not fully understand David's love of soccer, or even where it came from, but she responded to it, supported it, and nurtured it.

As a teen, my sister displayed an interest in luxury items like high-end handbags, clothes from couture labels, and exquisite jewelry. Our mom was less interested in such things and wanted to encourage responsible spending in her children. She wasn't sure if Nora's interest was truly deep or rather

58 · RAISING GRITTY KIDS

was rooted in a need to meet pressure from friends who used conspicuous consumption to signal status.

Mom did not necessarily want to discourage Nora if she was truly interested in the quality and workmanship required to craft these goods. She understood that on some level, this was a matter of preference. She might not share it with my sister, but she could understand and appreciate it as a legitimate choice.

Whenever Nora asked our mom to buy a name-brand item, Mom did not immediately say no. Instead she would say something like, "I will give you the amount that I would pay for a purse for you. If you want a name-brand purse, you can save money from your allowance to make up the difference." That is responsive parenting. Mom responded to Nora's interest, but she also demanded responsible behavior, teaching my sister the value of money and hard work in the process. My sister's response was to go to our local mall and apply for a job at the boutique that carried her favorite designers. She was able to lock in the employee discount and buy the clothes and handbags that she wanted.

PUSHING FOR GROWTH WITHOUT BREAKING

How does one make age-appropriate demands that are also attuned to the specific needs of the child? The way to cultivate growth and a sense of responsibility in a healthy manner is to allow the child to push his boundaries of capability while communicating his needs and preferences in the situation. The ideal is when the goal is just out of reach and there is the possibility of "failing" in the effort, but never of being irreparably crushed by the experience. This requires that the parent know the child, pay close attention to the trajectory of emotion she is experiencing, and course correct with words of encouragement and wisdom when necessary.

One of our mom's mantras was, "If you start something, you must finish it." When David wanted to play soccer at a competitive level, our mom put in the time and money to help him pursue it, but she also wanted to know that he was going to see it through to a reasonable end. She did not want to invest the time and effort and have him quit in a year. Little did she know what she was encouraging! Having watched David recover from many serious injuries over the years, our mom has said she is more than ready for him to give up the soccer bug.

Although our mom always encouraged us to see whatever we started through to a reasonable conclusion, if we could convince her that we had really tried, but were no longer interested, that was okay.

For a while, my sister was studying violin as well as beginning gymnastics. She really fell in love with gymnastics, and was training up to three hours after school many days a week. That left little time for her to practice violin. My sister pleaded her case and Mom agreed to let her quit music, in large part because she knew her child. She knew Nora was not simply trying to get out of music. Nora did stick with gymnastics and became very competitive on the uneven bars, winning some regional competitions. It turned out that the violin lessons were not in vain either. My sister still plays on special occasions at the church where she is pastor.

When my brother was about five years old, our mom started

him in violin lessons. By the time he was nine, he was already expressing his preference for soccer pretty vehemently. Our mom encouraged him to stick with violin until he could play in an orchestra. She thought he might enjoy playing with others more than playing solo.

David hit a final breaking point his freshman year in high school. Our mom had driven him to his weekly lesson, and shortly after arriving, the conversation in the car got tense. David refused to go inside. For years now, he had tried to juggle two demanding extracurricular activities, both of which required hours of practice. He had come to resent the time violin was taking away from his real love, soccer. He protested forcefully and announced, "No more violin lessons." At this point, he had made his preference known and our mom, respecting his budding autonomy in this space, acquiesced.

I hated sports and physical activity because I felt awkward and out of place, but I loved playing violin. I wanted to learn the most challenging pieces, sit in the first violin section of the prestigious youth orchestra in town, and maybe even one day become concertmistress. Truth be told, I also may have dreaded violin lessons from time to time. In my case, it was because I knew it was going to be challenging and my teacher was brutally honest about my musical shortcomings. However, I had my motivations and so I powered through. My brother did not, and once he had made his case, my parents let him stop so he could focus on soccer.

BEWARE PARENTAL OVERREACH

One clarifying point needs to be made here: parental responsiveness does not mean doing everything for the child. This kind of intensive or helicopter parenting in which parents make all the decisions and intervene inappropriately on behalf of the child could actually thwart the development of resiliency. Maria Montessori asks:

> Have you seen a fifteen year old child being carried in arms? This may not be done physically but parents and teachers are doing the same thing mentally, morally and figuratively in several aspects belonging to the child. Such help is unthinking unkindness. It is a hindrance.[18]

Helicopter parenting is characterized by low demandingness for age-appropriate maturity and high demandingness for things like achievement and performance. High responsiveness coupled with low demandingness in maturity can actually lead to lower levels of achievement, less self-regulation, and reduced social responsibility. Yes, parents should be responsive, but they also need the high-demanding piece to encourage responsible and mature behavior in their child.

Knowing the balance and specific action to take depends on the child. The example with my sister's interest in luxury goods illustrates this balance. Our mom acknowledged Nora's preferences and was responsive to them by not making Nora wrong for wanting designer labels. However, Mom also encouraged responsibility for those preferences by requiring Nora to make up the difference in price by working and saving to afford her purchases.

One sneaky place where helicopter parenting can show up is an overreach of advocacy for one's children. When parents constantly step in as a proxy—for example, telling the teacher, "It's unfair that my child got a bad grade. How are we going to

62 · RAISING GRITTY KIDS

fix that?"—it can be detrimental to the long-term well-being of the child. Advocacy that undermines the child's autonomy and self-confidence is not healthy advocacy. Keeping age-appropriate guidelines in mind, parents should give their child plenty of opportunities to self-advocate and to navigate progressively challenging interactions on their own.

At the same time, there are occasions where it is entirely appropriate for the parent to step in. When my brother was six years old, a little girl in his class thought he was cute and wrote him a sweet little love letter. The teacher, after intercepting the note, asked David about it. My brother explained that the girl had approached him, not the other way around. The teacher accused him of lying, and David was sent to the office, where he had to write a hundred times, "I am a liar. I will never lie again."

That same year, someone in David's class had a birthday celebration. Per class tradition, the students sat in a circle with the birthday girl in the center, and then students took turns serving cake to their classmates. When a student came to my brother, he said he did not want any because he didn't care for cake. The teacher pulled him out of the circle and made him stand in the corner. She could not fathom that a little boy would turn down the chance for sugary-sweet birthday cake. And again, she accused him of lying.

After that incident, my brother's spirit was more than a little bruised. David was a cooperative and polite child, but he also knew his preferences and was confident enough to voice them. However, at six years old, he did not have the tools to navigate the substantial power imbalance between himself and the teacher. Seeing how this incident impacted him, our mom stepped in.

In my brother's case, age-appropriate maturity was at play. Our mom taught us all to be respectful of teachers and authority figures, but also to know our own boundaries and preferences. David did not yet have the skills to have a conversation with his teacher to defend himself, but he was able to tell our mom what happened. Our mom knew he was not a liar and went to bat for him. Ultimately, after a few more incidents like this, our mom also knew that this school was not the right fit for my brother, and she found him a new place to attend.

Advocacy is suitable when your child does not have the age-appropriate skills to deal with a situation. If the child is old enough to have those skills, then you can gift her the opportunity to work it out on her own—even if that means letting her try and fail.

KNOW YOUR CHILD TOOL KIT

Here are a few suggestions for getting to know your child and developing your responsive parenting skills.

READ

Maria Montessori offers an excellent resource for parents of young children zero to four years old: *What You Should Know About Your Child*. You can read it online for free through Open Library. This book has excellent points to consider—and discuss with your partner and other parents—related to how you are nurturing your children to be autonomous.

REVISIT YOUR LANDSCAPE

Think about who in your environment is a true advocate

64 · RAISING GRITTY KIDS

for your child. I say "true" here because the notion of age-appropriate advocacy extends beyond parents to anyone who might be speaking up for the child. It is good to have others watching out for the well-being of your child, especially in situations where you cannot be present.

Advocates, those who acknowledge the child's autonomy and give opportunities for self-expression and agency, can show up in the most unlikely places. When I broke my arm at five years old, the brilliant and caring pediatric orthopedic surgeon who believed me when I said I could stay in traction for those long weeks ended up being the best advocate I could have hoped for in that situation.

OBSERVE THE SPECTRUM OF PERSONALITIES

Understanding and knowing your child requires deep thought about the nuanced personality traits your child might be exhibiting. Read biographies. Watch documentaries or biographical films. Talk to relatives and friends. All of these activities can deepen your understanding of the wide range of personality traits that human beings are capable of displaying—infinite combinations of generosity, shyness, manipulation, selfishness, drive, overt aggressiveness, attention seeking, passivity, confidence, and much more.

Documentaries and biographies feature real people struggling with real issues. In watching and reading, you have a chance to see how people navigated the world given their unique makeup, which might provide ideas for shepherding your own child in realistic ways. Understanding people, with their defining personality characteristics, is especially helpful if you and your partner do not share the traits you see in your child.

KNOW YOUR CHILD · 65

The reality is that most people hope to see themselves in their children, a kind of mini-me, so to speak. This does not always happen, and the child that is decidedly different deserves to be understood and loved. An example might be very extroverted parents with an introverted child. Another example could be individuals who find themselves parenting a polymath or prodigy. Or very analytical parents who have a child that is more intuitive. Or very physically attractive parents whose child is less so.

Finally, you might also read biographies involving parents and children, or simply watch those around you as they parent. While doing so, observe how different parents interact with their children and what strategies they use. Would your child respond to a similar technique? Borrowing a good idea is an excellent idea.

TAILOR YOUR PARENTING

Some children crave the approval of parents. Some are more defiant and willing to endure a reprimand. It is wise to be aware of these two extremes in order to understand the emotional needs of the young child. Sometimes, the behavior that was tolerated as cutesy when the child was small can become a headache in the teen years. What has happened in this case?

On the other hand, a child who appears shy and overhears a parent regularly making apologies for that behavior, ironically, may go through a period of self-consciousness, fearing further disapproval. The parent must consider how to encourage self-confidence, which is an important tool as the child discovers that his choices and preferences might actually diverge from those of the parents. It is this early process of differentiation

66 · RAISING GRITTY KIDS

that will ensure that one day the child will stand on his own. The adventurous spirit is important to nurture, because from that ultimately springs the potential for resilience.

Novels and short stories can provide glimpses of realistic characters with well-defined personality traits, thriving and surviving during times of shifting landscapes. A parent might read stories like those by early twentieth-century novelist Edna Ferber, while developing a parenting style tailored for a particular child. Getting to know Ferber's characters offers food for thought. There are classic children's stories, too, that are both entertaining and full of myriad characters whose traits can easily become parent-child conversation opportunities.

An excellent example is *Wind in the Willows* by Kenneth Grahame. In this story we find Mole, Toad, Rat, and Badger entertainingly responding to various circumstances and landscapes. When reading with children, the first experience should be just for fun—no questions, no criticism. After an initial reading, the parent might ask easy questions: Was Mole having a problem? Was he unhappy? Why did he want to leave home? What do you think of Toad? Of course, there are no right answers. As parents, you can simply relax, listen, and enjoy the child's point of view.

At the end of an eighth-grade graduation ceremony at the school where I worked, students were handed a lifetime reading list, which in my opinion at the time was a very thoughtful gesture. And it was. It included marvelous storytellers like Jane Austen, F. Scott Fitzgerald, Joseph Conrad, Fyodor Dostoevsky, and Agatha Christie.

Several years later, however, I realized that some cultures were not represented on the list. Today I believe that in order to craft an original, specifically tailored parenting style, reading should be relevant to the immediate family and also reflect the diversity, both ethnically and socioeconomically, of the greater culture. My revised lifetime reading list would include books like *Mulberry Child* by Jian Ping, *Stand Up Straight and Sing!* by Jessye Norman, the Studs Lonigan trilogy by James Farrell, *Chicago: City on the Make* by Nelson Algren, *So Big* by Edna Ferber, *Find Where the Wind Goes* by Mae Jemison, and *Arctic Dreams* by Barry Lopez. For young children specifically, consider *Niño Wrestles the World* by Yuyi Morales, *Journey to Jo'Burg* by Beverley Naidoo, and the *Random House Book of Poetry for Children*.

WELL-BALANCED CHILD

Our organic parenting style is bidirectional. It's a path of communication between parent and child that balances demandingness and responsiveness in a way that honors the child's unique personality while fostering mature, responsible behavior.

To encourage growth without injuring the child's self-confidence and self-esteem, parents should get to know the child's innate preferences, strengths, and weaknesses across the mental, physical, emotional, social, and spiritual domains. In the next five chapters, we discuss these different aspects in turn while focusing on the role of each in raising gritty kids. We do not believe that your child must develop these facets equally or even in a prescribed way. But we do want to offer ways for you to observe and engage with the facets that make your child unique.

Recognizing that personality traits may be more tendency than set path, each chapter provides tools for helping your child try on new behaviors, test responses, and work toward constructive habits and skills. Understanding strengths and weaknesses, identifying areas that need to be developed, and practicing self-acceptance through it all will put your child on the path to being well balanced and productive. Our first concern, as Suzuki said, "is the importance of educating a really beautiful human spirit."[19]

CHAPTER 3

Nurturing Mental Interests

"The foundation of education must be based on the following facts: That the joy of the child is in accomplishing things great for his age; that the real satisfaction of the child is to give maximum effort to the task in hand; that happiness consists in well directed activity of body and mind in the way of excellence; that strength of mind and body and spirit is acquired by exercise and experience; and that true freedom has, as its objective, service to society and to mankind consistent with the progress and happiness of the individual.

"The freedom that is given to the child is not liberation from parents and teachers; it is not freedom from the laws of nature or of the state or society but the utmost freedom for self-development and self-realisation compatible with service to society."

—MARIA MONTESSORI, *WHAT YOU SHOULD KNOW ABOUT YOUR CHILD*

Some children groom their stuffed animals, engage them in elaborate tea parties, and ensure they are comfortably tucked in at night. Not me. As a child of five or six, I played bank with my Care Bears, treating them as customers, some with questionable credit worthiness.

My bank had an elaborate setup, beyond having a piggy bank with coins I had saved. This was high finance: determining lending risk, deciding which projects were worthy of a loan, dictating how much money my playmates could borrow, and above all, making sure they paid it back.

My mom recognized my interest and let me gather the deposit slips when we went to the bank. This was before ATMs were ubiquitous and you still had to go to a teller, slip in hand, to deposit money or check your balances. When I was a little older, she would send me into the bank alone to pay the mortgage. While she waited in the car on a busy downtown Chicago street, I would enter the bank and stand in line with the businessmen, holding the mortgage slip and check. When it was my turn, I would walk up to the counter and, standing on tippy toes, slide the payment across and wait patiently for the receipt. Barely tall enough to make eye contact with the teller, I still felt right at home.

Where did my interest come from? Our family is made up of engineers, medical researchers, academics, professors, and teachers. We do not have any bankers in the family, at least, not in the formal sense. Yet my fascination with finance was strong then and continues to this day.

My daughter, on the other hand, is artistically inclined and very interested in dance and performance. She absolutely loves *Peter and the Wolf, The Nutcracker*, and *Marian Anderson and Her Snoopycat.*

During the holiday season before Lena turned three, I introduced her to a family tradition: watching *The Nutcracker* in the days before Christmas. She really took to it and we ended up watching *The Nutcracker* every night for about three months. Well into the new year, we were still watching. We would watch forty-five minutes one night and then come back and finish it the next. Every night. For three months.

What caught my attention was the intensity with which Lena watched the production. She studied how the dancers moved. She observed the detail of their costumes. She wanted to understand what was happening and why. After watching it so many times, Lena started enacting the dances, pulling my husband and me into her toddler's interpretation of the Sugar Plum Fairy.

She did the same thing with *Peter and the Wolf*, Prokofiev's symphonic story for children in which each character is associated with a particular instrument. At a young age, Lena was able to identify the characters by their leitmotifs. She recognized the bird played by the flute, the clarinet as the cat, Peter by the strings, and the wolf by the ominous French horns.

After picking up on her keen interest, and to mix things up a bit, we started watching different versions of both productions so she could compare and contrast. With *The Nutcracker*, Lena could articulate which choreography she liked better and which costumes she preferred (the 2012 Mariinsky Ballet version is her favorite). With *Peter and the Wolf*, we found one with dancing (the 1995 Royal Ballet version), which she

NURTURING MENTAL INTERESTS · 73

adored because it had it all—the music, the story, glorious costumes, *and* she got to dance. At a certain point, she knew *Peter and the Wolf* so well that she could repeat the narration from memory.

On Memorial Day sometime later, we attended a family barbecue. After everyone had finished eating, Lena said, "Let's do *Peter and the Wolf!*" She assigned everyone parts: my brother was Peter, my dad was the wolf, I was the grandfather, and Lena was the bird, because the bird gets to flit around everywhere antagonizing the duck, the cat, and the wolf with her fleet-footed moves.

Not everyone knew the story, so Lena walked them through, saying things like, "Well, here's what's going to happen and here's what you're going to do." She was the only child at the barbecue, and here she was directing an impromptu production with all the adults dutifully following her instructions and getting into their roles.

Understanding finance and memorizing lyrics and dance steps fall into what we call mental interests, which are not to be confused with more traditional forms of academics. Every child is born with unique gifts and talents, and the parent's first task is determining what those are through careful observation and conversation. Once these talents are identified, parents can then provide opportunities to delve deeper, improve, and expand understanding in ways that develop other qualities—self-confidence, perseverance, autonomy—that in turn contribute to resiliency.

In this chapter, we want to turn the discussion around mental capabilities away from more narrow definitions of achieve-

74 · RAISING GRITTY KIDS

ment and focus instead on the joy of learning. We will share ways to seize the areas to which the child is naturally drawn to encourage curiosity, lifelong learning, and more.

DIVERGENT THINKING AND A GROWTH MINDSET

Maria Montessori, ahead of her time in myriad ways, foretold an education system that papers over children's unique talents rather than embracing them. Montessori's suggestion through her methods and books was to get out of the way and learn to appreciate the special gifts each person possesses. In this way, we help society deeply by allowing children to learn and grow organically into well-balanced adults who find joy in work and through positive effort.

The foundation for this chapter is to seek out at least one area to which your child is naturally drawn, where you can observe, facilitate, and ultimately get out of the way to the let the child explore freely and primarily for the pleasure of learning. More traditional views of academic achievement have their place. However, if the ongoing lack of consensus from researchers about what constitutes intelligence is any indication, it need not be the only focus in childhood development.

People now recognize that the convergent thinking and learning that worked in the past may no longer be the best path to fostering a lifelong love of learning and a commitment to creative problem-solving skills relevant to building resilience. Today, society as a whole is more accepting of the idea that there are many types of intelligence. Pop psych and business leadership articles alike regularly reference the importance of emotional and social intelligence in long-term success.

We take the practical view that the skills for successfully navigating life's challenges can be developed within various intellectual domains, many of which are outside of the classroom. Aligning that aim with what is of interest to the child is one way to make learning more enjoyable and self-driven. For the purposes of developing resiliency, we believe it is important to focus on divergent thinking and a growth mindset, not their opposites.

Convergent thinking is more linear and systematic. A lot of school learning today tends to be conducted and assessed in convergent thinking formats. Standardized, multiple-choice tests are a prime example. Divergent thinking, on the other hand, is more free-flowing and web-like, looking to make connections between ideas rather than settling on one, single correct answer.

In a rapidly changing environment, one is well served by incorporating divergent thinking in the life skills tool kit. It fosters the ability to take what one knows today and to apply that knowledge to new situations and environments. One needs to discern what is relevant, what is not, and to seek out creative, outside-the-box solutions. Someone who thinks primarily in a linear fashion may not be able to respond as quickly or efficiently when the landscape shifts around them.

Carol Dweck, the originator of the fixed-versus-growth-mindset discussion, asserts that a student with a fixed mindset believes that his basic abilities, intelligence, and talents are fixed traits. A student with a growth mindset, on the other hand, believes his abilities and intelligence can be developed with effort, learning, and persistence. Fostering a growth mindset in children is crucial for developing resiliency and will enable them to navigate times of uncertainty more easily.

76 · RAISING GRITTY KIDS

NURTURING INTERESTS TO BUILD OTHER QUALITIES

As parents notice their child's unique interests and capabilities, they have an opportunity to nurture those gifts and foster growth in other areas.

In Lena's case, I understand that my daughter's personality and interests are still developing. She clearly has capability in music and dance, but it is too early to tell whether this will continue to be a core part of her makeup. What I do know is that today, Lena's intense interest provides an opportunity for me to connect with her and to champion curiosity, expertise, perseverance, and other important qualities for becoming a responsible, productive member of society.

Lena's explorations in music and dance have bolstered her self-confidence. In our house, she is the undisputed expert on *Peter and the Wolf.* As was illustrated at that long-ago family barbeque, her "studies" enabled her to impart her knowledge with authority and to enroll the adults in her vision for that impromptu production.

By watching *The Nutcracker* repeatedly, Lena, at age three, was already honing her skills of observation. With each viewing, she noticed new details and made connections between what she observed elsewhere. As a result, she formed a well-reasoned opinion, with supporting evidence, as to why the Mariinsky Ballet was her favorite.

Developing an eye for detail in this manner takes time and persistence. Lena did not listen to *Peter and the Wolf* one time. At her request, we listened to it repeatedly. Her commitment resulted in expertise, to the extent that even as a three-year-old, her ears perked up when she heard the opening chords of Peter's theme, transformed into lite-listening muzak, as we sat in the dentist's waiting room.

That next Christmas season, I decided to plan a mini-vacation centered on Lena's interest. We traveled four hours by train to a nearby city to see a live production of *The Nutcracker* as well as spend hours exploring the lovely outdoor holiday market. Although I do not recall thinking this at the time, I imagine children Lena's age might unconsciously feel like little people in their parents' household, taking up space but not really having the same importance. By planning that trip, I hoped to give Lena the sense in real terms that her interests are important, that I support her dedication to learning, and that I am interested in hearing what she has to say and how she is experiencing the world.

No matter what your child's interest, it is important to praise effort, rather than natural ability. The goal is to encourage curiosity, starting with the areas toward which the child already gravitates and then adding new and unfamiliar territory along the way. The more your child associates learning and development with positive feelings, the more likely she will grow into a lifelong learner, unafraid to develop new skills and adapt to changes in the landscape.

Autonomy and self-management are two other essential qualities you can nurture with this approach. By focusing on an area in which your child already has an interest, she will be self-driven in a more natural way. From here, the child more easily slips into a state of flow, unthinking of time and engaged in the activity for the sheer enjoyment of it. Parents can use a deep experience of self-directed effort and accomplishment as a springboard to a more general appreciation for the fruits

78 · RAISING GRITTY KIDS

of persistence. Once firmly established, you can introduce other modalities as potential areas for new exploration.

Here is a concrete example. My childhood play as resident banker was a tad cold and calculating. I enjoyed doling out my decisions about who got what. And at my bank there was no appeals process. It might have been a teachable moment to introduce a discussion about equity and the common good with a question like, "Are there projects that don't give a big financial return that you still might support because they're good for the whole community?" Use the child's love as a launching point to discuss other areas that are worth exploring.

What if your child's interest is vastly different from your own? Or suppose you have an interest, but your child has advanced beyond your capability to develop and foster the skill further? To nurture the child's interest, it can be a great gift to help find a proxy, a kindred spirit, as it were, willing and capable of suggesting paths to the next level of understanding.

Because of our interest in science growing up, our mom held family memberships at both the Museum of Science and Industry and the Adler Planetarium. From a young age, my brother and I attended lectures and participated in Science Club at MSI. I especially loved the annual sleepovers held at the planetarium. It felt vaguely verboten but so fun to stay up way past bedtime and explore the exhibits after dark.

One day, we received the usual quarterly brochure from the Adler. My brother found it, read about a sports physics workshop, and asked if he could go. He was nine years old at the time, and the workshop was for adults, but our mom, noticing

NURTURING MENTAL INTERESTS · 79

how strong his interest was, called the organizers and was told he could attend.

The event was led by a physics instructor from a local college. David was the only child in attendance, but he followed along and asked questions about momentum and the trajectory of the ball, soccer balls in particular. Our mom, who had decided to attend the class with him, realized through his questioning that he had an exceptional knowledge of the application of principles in physics. Until then, she had not fully realized he knew as much as he did. It was a great experience because in that one-day course, David got to explore both physics and soccer with teachers who could deepen his knowledge in meaningful ways.

This story illustrates a couple of important things. First, our mom recognized David's interest in physics and soccer, and she found others who could support and encourage his continued growth. Second, she was willing to go outside of the typical prescribed spaces to seek out these proxies.

Sometimes as adults we decide where children should or should not be. I felt that way with my daughter and *The Nutcracker*. Before I bought the tickets, I wondered if perhaps she was too young to attend an actual ballet, even one aimed at children. In truth, Lena sat on the edge of her seat, watching the dancers, rapt with attention. That being said, a little sensitivity to a situation goes a long way. Don't torture your child and other attendees at a museum or concert where absolute quiet is required. Many such places have created special spaces or events for young children in particular.

A common theme in this book is to be open to what your child brings. When parents acknowledge the validity of a young child's interests and capabilities, they help the child develop self-esteem. When that affirmation does not happen, self-doubt can creep in and the child may become more vulnerable to external opinions and expectations.

THE CHILD'S POINT OF VIEW

My mother wrote this poem following a family trip to Florida, during which she took a young grandson to see the manatees.

The Manatee
She swam; the baby swam
She swam; the baby swam
Side by side in the murky waters
Of the Crystal River, they swam
Effortlessly, tirelessly, gracefully
They swam; the Mama manatee
And her calf.

Were they talking to each other,
Serious mother/daughter talk?
Were they laughing, kidding,
Or just "kicking it" while gently gliding
Up and down and down and up the lagoon
Dipping and swirling; their huge forms
Barely visible to the naked eye.

We'll never know what their conversation
Was about. Will we?
At bedtime, the little child, half asleep now,
Wondered aloud "Pa-Pa, where do
The manatee sleep?"[20]

How can we really know what is going on in the mind of the child? As parents, we often assume that our POV (point of view, as writers say), is the child's POV. When a young David asked to attend the sports physics seminar, I assumed it indicated a rather precocious interest in math and science. This was true to some extent. However, it wasn't until now when, as an adult, he shared that attending the seminar came with his hope to learn strategies to sharpen his soccer skills.

His passion for soccer persists to this day. Interestingly, in just the way that COVID-19 changed things for everybody, David's adult league games were suspended. Yet he found a way to bring a bit of soccer home in these challenging times. I was hardly surprised when David texted a picture of the elaborate Lego replica he had just completed of Old Trafford, the stadium of Manchester United, his all-time favorite "football" team. In a conversation with my insightful sister, she commented, "Not only soccer, but the physics of structures using Legos!"

. . . .

TOOL KIT FOR NURTURING MENTAL INTERESTS

Hopefully, by now we have established that we are not talking about traditional academic programs. We are talking about potential areas of interest and capability for your child, as well as opportunities for collaborative exploration between you and your child. This tool kit provides ideas for finding and nurturing your child's unique talents, interests, and gifts.

As a parent, guard against the temptation to decide for the child that one of these areas is now going to be the primary focus. Seeing that your child may have an early interest along some potentially profitable vector can be exciting, especially for a parent focused on the future professional success of the child. However, try to simply enjoy the opportunity to connect with your child and nurture her preference. It should not be a chore, for you or your child. And always keep in mind that the interests you see today may not persist.

In summary, our guiding principle for nurturing mental interest in young children is to take time to observe, without comment or interference. Simply watch and listen. Be assured your child will learn the ABCs and much more. As Maria Montessori has said, a teacher has to trust that the child will reveal himself through the work. When the child reveals what he is interested in, you can respond with "Tell me more…" and think through how to engage with your child in that activity.

The following is not an exhaustive list, but it will get you started.

MATH/COMPUTER SCIENCE/LOGIC/ENGINEERING

Some children naturally gravitate toward numbers, science, and engineering. Principles of math theory can be found throughout the natural environment. In the very young child, this can manifest as observing symmetry in nature, recognizing cause-effect relationships, or classifying objects and noting the relationships between them. Taking time to acknowledge these observations is one way to encourage the child to share more.

Here are some suggestions for nurturing this interest in older kids:

- *What Is the Name of This Book? The Riddle of Dracula and Other Logical Puzzles* by Raymond Smullyan. When my siblings and I were young, we brought this classic logic puzzle book with us when we went out for Friday night pizza dinners. As we waited for the piping-hot pies to arrive at our table, we had great fun tackling the puzzles together, using our paper placemats as impromptu scratch pads to determine who was a knight and who was a knave.

- Code.org. Recommended by a friend who is a world-class programmer and is using this site with his children, it offers hours of free, educational fun. As soon as your child is able to read, introduce her to Code.org to see if she has an interest.
- Raspberry Pi. If your child shows an interest in engineering and tinkering with computers in particular, check out Raspberry Pi, which gives children the opportunity to build and program their own desktop computer for under forty dollars.
- Khan Academy. Even if you have a fear or dislike of math, things can be different for your child. There are many excellent resources online that explain math concepts in fun and accessible ways. Khan Academy is wonderful, free, and offers lessons in all the typical school subjects as well as math-based life skills like personal finance and applying and paying for college.

VERBAL/LITERARY

Here are some suggestions for nurturing the word-loving child:

- The Art of Storytelling. This fantastic resource for children was developed by Mensa and can be found at https://www.mensaforkids.org/teach/lesson-plans/the-art-of-storytelling/. It provides step-by-step directions illustrating how to craft compelling stories, from fairy tales and folklore to personal anecdotes and beyond. Encourage your little one to make up a story and then share it with the family. Also, consider checking out a storytelling podcast like WBUR's *Circle Round*, which shares tales from many cultural traditions in a child-friendly format.

- Reading together regularly. This is important for all children as it provides consistent exposure to vocabulary. According to Jessica Logan, assistant professor of educational studies at The Ohio State University, "Kids who hear more vocabulary words…are likely to pick up reading skills more quickly and easily."[21] Even for older children, reading books and discussing together can be a wonderful way to bond and facilitate communication. Open Library is a free, online source for many classic books, accessible without leaving your home. If you have an internet connection, you can read books on your laptop, tablet, or phone. A visit to the local library to borrow physical books is a rite of passage for any young child. By letting your child make the selections, you can also get a sense of her interests.

ART/MUSIC/DANCE

More formal art classes and music lessons are always an option, but here are some ways to nurture an interest in art and music in your own home:

- Art box. Keep a box full of basic art supplies so your budding artist can create to his heart's content: colored paper of various weights, plain white paper, glue and glue sticks, stickers, markers, pencils, scissors, pom-poms, pipe cleaners, Popsicle sticks, and more. Including items that can be turned into anything encourages creativity and divergent thinking. Watch how your child uses supplies to craft something unique.

- Art kits. In addition to providing freeform items, you can offer art kits for tie-dying, making wooden bead jewelry, creating sticker mosaics, making painted rock friends, and more. Your child will experience the great sense of accomplishment that comes from overseeing a project from start to finish.

- Dance like no one is watching. I am a big believer in listening to all sorts of music with Lena. We have regular weekend afternoon dance parties where we blast all manner of music. Sometimes we mix it up, and sometimes there is a specific genre on offer. It might be Motown one time, then K-pop next, and hard bop after that. There's never a dull moment when parent and child hit the living room dance floor together.

- Make your own musical instruments. A little parental creativity goes a long way here. Lena and I have taken soup cans and turned them into shakers, trying out different contents to see how the sound changes. An empty coffee can or oatmeal container can make a great drum. Make a kazoo out of a paper tube, rubber band, and some wax paper. Then, bring your instruments to the aforementioned dance party and watch out!

ECONOMICS AND BUSINESS

If your child is interested in economics and business, the following activities are practical and can be great fun too:

- Playing grocery store. There are child-sized grocery sets complete with play money you can buy for relatively cheap. Or you can repurpose empty containers before you recycle or throw them out; just make sure they are appropriately sized for small hands to manage. You can incorporate math into your play as well, as your child tallies the bill and makes change. After playing grocery store at home, you can take the game into real life. For example, have children guesstimate the total price of the items in the cart and see how close they come to the actual total.

- Budgeting. This exercise can be a good way to stave off drama at the checkout counter. Next time you go to a store where your child might want to buy something, give him a set amount of money and tell him that he can buy whatever he wants for that amount. This provides a great opportunity to explore the concepts of value versus cost and understanding trade-offs ("If I buy X, then I don't have enough for Y"). Finally, holding money, physically handing it to the cashier, and receiving and counting the change all provide your child with a sense of autonomy.
- Econedlink.org. The Council for Economic Education offers the free, downloadable *Family-At-Home Financial Fun Pack*, filled with activities for K–12. This online program introduces children to a wide range of economic concepts, from saving and borrowing to taxes and the basics of entrepreneurship.
- Field trips. When you plan family vacations, consider visiting places like the US Mint or the Federal Reserve Bank nearest you. When I was about eleven years old, I had the opportunity to visit the Chicago Board of Trade, back when brokers still clamored over one another in the pits, yelling out trades and using their distinctive hand signals to indicate price, quantity, and more. It remains a vivid memory to this day, one that probably influenced my decision to spend a college summer working at the Board of Trade, and much later, to pursue a career in derivatives trading.

FRAMEWORKS/PHILOSOPHY

Some people are interested in how we learn, how we think, and the connections between ideas. Others love to think about ethics and how we decide what is right and wrong. If your child falls in this category, try the following activities to encourage divergent thinking and foster this interest:

- Critical Learning Companion. Created by Wabisabi Learning, this critical thinking companion is an excellent tool for encouraging divergent thinking in school age children. If you were educated in a school that emphasized more rote learning methods, you might not know how to encourage divergent thinking in your child. You can draw on resources such as the Critical Learning Companion to help initiate discussions around this kind of learning.
- Philosophy for Children. University of Washington's Center for Philosophy for Children has resources for parents and grandparents to engage with children on philosophical topics like fear and worry, boredom, how do we know what we know, social equity, and more. They also provide a list of over one hundred children's books with discussion guides to explore philosophical questions. Find it at https://www.philosophyforchildren.org/resources/questions-library/.

HISTORY

Some children are fascinated by history, whether familial, local, or global. The following activities can help foster this interest:

- Family stories. As we have discussed in the preceding chapters, sharing family history is especially grounding for children. It lets them know that they are a part of a larger family unit, one that has its own unique legacy. Talking about family history also can provide a springboard for conversation with your child about what values you hold and why. Finally, consider that you and your immediate family are literally making your own history. You can employ some of the storytelling principles from the Mensa website to reminisce on a memorable family event. For instance, Lena had great fun recounting to my mom and dad the details of a recent trip to an old-school amusement park. We still laugh and talk about all the frightening rides we took and the giant dragon with the glittering red eyes that scared even me.

- Museums. It can be great to spend a weekend afternoon visiting a local museum. Many, natural history and otherwise, offer classes or other opportunities for children to be mentored by museum professionals. This is especially helpful if the child is interested in an area with which parents are not familiar or if the child's interest and aptitude go beyond the parents' own understanding and ability to foster. Do not discount what may be available at smaller museums. When I was about eight years old, I attended a mock archaeological dig at the Spertus Institute where we searched for artifacts that would inform us about Near Eastern history. Visiting the DuSable Museum was sobering even as a child, and provided hours of subsequent discussion about what I had seen.

"An unlimited amount of ability can develop when parent and child are having fun together."
—SHINICHI SUZUKI, *ABILITY DEVELOPMENT FROM AGE ZERO*

NURTURING MENTAL INTERESTS · 89

FOSTER CURIOSITY

As a parent, you have the opportunity to help your child develop a tool kit for lifelong learning and curiosity, which will help in navigating a shifting landscape. By meeting your child where she is, by building a common bridge and common language around the child's interests, you are putting her in a better position to develop the tools she needs to be resilient.

You will know you have succeeded in letting your child develop and explore his own intellectual interests when he loses himself in a state of flow. For some children, physical activities provide this place of engaged exploring. In the next chapter, we will consider the importance of movement in developing the whole child.

CHAPTER 4

Physicality and
Self-Esteem

*"Movement has great importance in mental development itself,
provided that the action which occurs is connected with the
mental activity going on. Both mental and spiritual growth
are fostered by this, without which neither maximum progress
nor maximum health can exist."*

—MARIA MONTESSORI, *THE ABSORBENT MIND*

Every child will gravitate toward one of the five facets of
individuality, and others will be of less interest or even
an outright struggle. Without doubt, physical well-being
was the area I wrestled most with through childhood and
beyond.

I was a plump child by today's standards, at the outer edges
of overweight and in some years probably closer to medi-
cally obese. At the dreaded annual check-up, the pediatrician
would often suggest to my mom that enrolling me in more
physical activities would be a good idea. I hated those reminders that I was plumper than almost every one of my peers.

PHYSICALITY AND SELF-ESTEEM · 91

And the aforementioned activities felt more like torture than for my well-being.

These early weight struggles had many consequences when it came to my self-esteem and confidence. My mom tried to reframe my weight issues in positive terms, calling me "pleasingly plump," and as I grappled with teenage insecurities, she noted that some guys preferred women with a little meat on their bones. Still, as I looked out into a world where the most successful and desirable women that I knew were thinner, if not entirely thin, I felt painfully out of sync.

My early role models of femininity were mostly svelte and slender. My grandmother and great-aunts, who were striking beauties, shopped at Neiman Marcus and Saks Fifth Avenue for sharp, tailored outfits I could only dream of wearing. They were perfect size 4s with tiny feet to boot.

My mother, who used to joke self-deprecatingly that she had skinny twig legs, was a perpetual object of male interest. I watched guys hit on her at the gas station, the grocery store, and my music lessons, in spectacularly forward fashion, while I gazed on, longing to be seen by a boy, any boy.

I have a particularly vivid memory of my mom attending a school field trip with my seventh-grade class. Because we were leaving a little later in the morning, my mom had agreed to meet us at the school.

I remember sitting on the bus that fine spring morning, windows down, chatter all around. Out of the corner of my eye, I saw my mom walking down the sidewalk toward the bus. She was wearing a lovely summer dress slightly below the knees, by no means outwardly sexy or flashy.

At that moment, I heard some of my male classmates whistling. I turned to see them hanging their heads out the window, staring at my mom.

"Who's that?" one of them asked with awe.

"Dude, she's a fox!" another responded.

Excuse me? I thought. *That's my mom!* I felt a strange mix of horror, pride, and jealousy.

Needless to say, I spent more than a little time preoccupied with how I looked, how I showed up in the world, and how I compared to others.

In the end, things have worked out okay for me in the physical realm. I developed a more balanced relationship with food and exercise. I managed to run half and full marathons, although I was initially drawn to running through a volunteer opportunity to mentor at-risk teens while racking up dozens of miles along the Chicago lakefront.

I also developed a love of hiking and being in the outdoors. My first camping excursion took me to King George Island off the coast of Antarctica, where I spent seven days hiking miles at a time over glaciers and up craggy ridges with a fifty-pound pack strapped to my back. I have gradually come to a sort of truce with my physical presence. Still, with slightly different tools when I was younger, my self-perception and self-esteem may have been less impacted.

PHYSICALITY AND SELF-ESTEEM · 93

In this chapter, we will define physicality and its importance, provide a framework for thinking about physicality apart from athletic ability, and share tools for helping your child be comfortable in his skin.

UNDERSTANDING PHYSICALITY

What of us mere mortals who are more plain Jane than knock-out? Notions of physical attractiveness have come a long way since when I was growing up. Today, there is increasing sensibility that all kinds of people, with their different shapes, tones, and features, can be beautiful in their own right. Parents have a powerful opportunity to reframe the context around physical presence so that children can grow to have a healthy view of physicality, physical ability, and self-perception.

To that end, here are a few introductory thoughts about physicality and its importance in your child's wholeness as a person. If this list seems almost mantra-like, in fact, it is. These are the very thought patterns I worked to adopt in order to interrupt my negative self-talk about my body.

- The physical body is important for practical reasons. It helps us move around in the world. It enables us to go to work, dine with friends, attend concerts, and travel the world. For that reason, the body is a worthy assistant in helping us meet our aims.
- When people are physically active, they experience very real physical and chemical reactions that provide a resiliency advantage. In general, physically active people manage stress better and regulate emotions better, both of which are necessary for navigating uncertain situations.

- As Maria Montessori says, "The hands are the instruments of man's intelligence."[22] People learn by actually doing, and in doing, people develop confidence that they can do even more. In addition, when people feel confident in the ability to do certain things, they are more likely to go outside of their comfort zone and try unfamiliar endeavors—all important for developing resiliency.

- Today's culture tends to focus on physical appearance, and although it is healthy to appreciate beauty for its aesthetic value, one must recognize that the vast majority of humans do not fall into the "great beauty" category. For children, who are all beautiful in their innocence and verve for life, it is wise early on to place beauty, physical in particular, in the context of something larger. It can be helpful to emphasize that bodies are wonderful tools to help people meet their aims in the world.

I regularly share with my daughter the awe with which I regard the workings of our bodies, and how little we do to keep our bodies running and humming along. It is a gift to have the freedom to focus on mental, emotional, and spiritual pursuits rather than maintaining the physical body, because so many autonomic functions—breathing, digestion, healing—are handled in the background. This means children's bodies, like everyone else's, are wonderful and worthy of care and love regardless of shape, size, appearance, and capability.

Physicality starts with one's literal body, but beyond that, it involves how one shows up in the world, how one navigates through the world and uses the body to accomplish things, and how all these bodies in the world relate to one another. At a personal level, having good boundaries promotes a sense of self-empowerment, which can safeguard against detrimental outside influences that make one feel less than.

· ·

TEENAGE SELF-CONCEPT

Within a few months of being away at college, my daughter and I started sharing poetry as a way to stay in touch. It was poems like the one below that revealed what she was going through:

Conviction
shame and guilt
that's no way to live
afraid and cowed
for what reason
because your voice is small
your conviction untested
how little they know
how much you'll know
there's nothing wrong
with you
or with feeling
out of place.

To me, this was a very coming-of-age message, a type of poetic bildungsroman. Of course, the mode of sharing may vary. Unusual choice of music, change in fashion or hairstyle, new diets that may include strange foods, are examples of ways that a young person may be trying to make sense of their place in the world, not actually asking for the parent's help, but attempting to communicate what can be the daunting experience of coming of age.

· ·

96 · RAISING GRITTY KIDS

FOSTERING SELF-ESTEEM

Many people, females especially, end up bruised or broken in this area of physical appearance, in part because they compare themselves to the media's airbrushed facades. Social media-driven comparison culture, with its apps for digitally enhancing your face, your body, your life, contributes to the pressure one might feel to fit a standard of beauty and physical perfection that is more tied to cultural preference than any objective measure. It is far too easy to internalize messages like, "I would be happy if I looked like that" or "I would have a boyfriend if I weren't overweight." As parents, you can help your children understand that looking a certain way does not guarantee happiness. There are plenty of drop-dead-gorgeous, utterly miserable people.

There are also long-term ramifications with equating one's value with the body and how the body appears. Even the most fit, handsome people age, add a little extra padding, and acquire some wrinkles—and that is okay. Instead of focusing on appearance, parents should try to encourage positive self-image that encompasses the body and more.

Many parents have their own baggage around the physical. This was certainly true for me. Having one's own insecurities can make it doubly hard to help a child in this area, but addressing them is potentially healing for both parent and child.

I am constantly on guard with my own self-talk to make sure I am not introducing things into Lena's space that I know are my own baggage. Beyond conceptions of weight, other areas of potentially harmful judgment that could be passed on to children include a focus on certain features like having the "right" kind of nose or even a preference for an "appropriate" height. Hair color, texture, and length is another place where subconscious bias can be passed along. In some cultures, care is taken not to get too brown or tan. When I was in the first grade, a close friend, coming out of such a culture, took a pencil eraser to my arm, and trying to erase my skin, asked cruelly, "How come you're so dark and dirty?"

Indeed, shifting the physicality conversation—from good and bad, desirable and objectionable, status raising and status diminishing—to one where we learn to love our bodies for what they allow us to do, can be positive not just for your child but for all the people with whom your child will interact.

REMEMBERING AUNT TEDDY

Anybody who has ever been a teenager knows that things start to happen to your body that are surprising, to say the least, and sometimes, plain old scary. In my case it was the hairs. Hairs that appeared where I'd hoped they would not. Hairs that kept one comedian's words repeatedly singing in my ears: "I've got little tiny hairs growing out of my face, little tiny hairs growing out of my face." The way he hummed it made you laugh, but he was old, and he was a man; he was supposed to have hairs on his face. A thirteen-year-old girl was not.

I showed my mother and she said, "What hairs?" But I saw them. Yes, it was happening. That could only mean I would have to use the stinky depilatory that my great-aunt used.

I loved and admired my great-aunt. She owned the six-flat building on Komensky Avenue, where our church was located. She let me work as a cashier in her corner store that was housed in the building, and she let me count all the change that accumulated in the cash register drawer. She was great, but she used Nair. The odor was worse than rotten eggs. I had seen her mix the powder to the proper consistency using a mortar and pestle. With each stir, the smell would waft through the air beyond the walls of her bathroom to assault the nostrils.

One day after I was sure that my future included the dreaded depilatory, I garnered the nerve to share my dire expectation. After all, I thought rather resolutely, it's best to learn now which steps must be taken once the hairs had taken over. I approached my great-aunt, and my tone pleaded for confidentiality: "I think I'm growing facial hair. Should I start buying Nair?"

She looked at me with wise and patient eyes, and then carefully said, "Let me take a good look at you." She came close and examined my cheeks and chin.

"Why do you have to use Nair?" I really wanted to know. It was worth a possible reprimand for being so forward with an adult. Nervously, I continued, "Is there anything else that maybe doesn't have that awful odor? Couldn't you just shave like my dad? Shaving cream is not so bad."

"No, baby," she said. "Don't ever use a razor on your tender skin. That will make the hairs grow back stronger and thicker."

She just said that would make the hairs grow, the hairs! I thought. *I knew she had seen them. I knew it! They were real. They were there!*

Even though the hairs were very fine and barely visible, Aunt Teddy confirmed what I suspected. No doubt, eventually the fine hairs would evolve into a bushy mustache and a big black beard.

Aunt Teddy interrupted my thoughts. "Let me tell you something, sweetie."

She confided, "First, do you know what *hirsute* means?" I didn't. "It's a condition that causes irregular hair growth." She leaned in close enough for me to see the deep pock marks on her face.

She continued, "It's called hirsutism. I have that condition. It is not really common. You may not even have it. It's probably that you're just growing up." She smiled.

Aunt Teddy was right. Over the years, despite occasional inspections in a well-lit mirror, the big, thick hairs never came.

• •

NURTURING PHYSICALITY TO BUILD OTHER QUALITIES

If the body is a means to get around and do things in the world, in concert with the mind and emotions, then it makes sense that the body can be used to strengthen abilities in these other areas. One can develop a physical practice that will sharpen concentration and increase the ability to focus during mental exertion.

One can also engage in physical activities that provide emotional and psychological resiliency. This is what happened when I trained with the at-risk teens for the Chicago Marathon. By showing up on a regular schedule to run during the week and on weekends, through cold spring rains and soaring summer temperatures, the teens experienced personal discipline in a visceral way. Through those long, hard training runs, we eventually reaped the benefits of our perseverance. When we crossed the finish line, there was the undeniable sense of accomplishment that comes from joining the ranks of the fewer than 1 percent of Americans who have completed a marathon. No one can take that experience away from those teens or the deep-in-the-bones knowledge of what is possible when working diligently with a long-term goal in sight. Finally, they learned an important truth about obstacles and hardship: they never last forever.

In terms of heightening a sense of self-confidence, such goal-oriented physical activity can be hard to beat. Acquiring mastery through repeated activity, children know when they are improving, when tasks become easier, and when their body is capable of doing more. The affirming feeling that comes from a focus on incremental improvement goes a long way in building self-esteem.

CURIOSITY AND BEING OKAY

My sister was a skilled gymnast who practiced two to three hours after school many days a week. She became quite adept on the uneven bars, winning a number of regional competitions. My brother was obsessed with soccer and gave up music to focus on his sport. I tried dance for a while, but I did not have a strong interest. When it came down to choosing, I opted for music over a more physical hobby. I simply was not interested in sports like my siblings were, and from my parents' perspective, that was okay.

However, for me, this disinterest morphed into a more serious kind of negative self-talk. It went beyond "this isn't something I'm interested in" and turned into "I can't do those kinds of things. It's not how I'm built."

If your child is slipping into this frame of thinking, try to reorient the conversation. Acknowledge that sports might not be your child's thing, but simultaneously encourage curiosity and a focus on trying. Instead of "I can't," the self-talk could be "with some willingness and effort, this is an area I could focus on and improve."

As an adult, I made a conscious decision to tackle the accumulated baggage of years of self-denigration. I decided to approach the project with the sense of curiosity I recommend above. Rather than decide at the outset that certain activities just were not for me, I decided to ask myself a series of what-if type questions. What would it be like to be a runner? What stores would I frequent that I never would have otherwise? How would my diet change? What kinds of physical discomforts would I encounter and have to mentally overcome? I was not sure of the answers to any of these when I started out, but I was willing to see the experiment through to the end. Much like the teens in the program, I was incredibly gratified to have had the experience. And in the end, I was a lot more fit too, and that was pretty cool in and of itself.

One final point to consider is that often parents and their children exhibit differing levels of ability in certain areas. Perhaps physical activity and sports come naturally to you, but not so for your own child, or vice versa. The important thing is to help your child accept where she is physically, avoid placing value-driven pressure related to performance ("You have to be a winner or you're nothing"), respect the child's interest or lack thereof, and help her maintain healthy self-esteem around what her body can do.

HOW WE SHOW UP

In terms of our physical bodies and appearance, there are

certain realities over which people have no control. A Black male in America cannot alter wholesale how people react or behave toward him. Other groups also find themselves the target of physically based stereotypes that can make it hard for individuals to express their truest selves.

As a parent, you have to be mindful of these realities and give your children tools to protect their own self-worth, regardless of outside influences. The unfortunate reality is that some people will make judgments based purely on how a child looks. This can be a painful moment to address, for both parent and child. Once immediate safety and well-being are assured, it is possible to address the more psychological impacts of such an encounter. Talk through what happened, try to understand the differing worldviews people have, and attempt to hold a space of compassion for those who make themselves feel better by trying to make others feel less than.

When children have healthy self-confidence and clear boundaries around self-perception, outside influences are less successful in penetrating or damaging their self-esteem. However, there are still times when the unequivocal reassurance of a caring figure is needed. When the child feels loved, lovable, and capable of being loving, even in the face of unfair treatment, that is the best shield against the negative influences of the world.

TOOL KIT FOR NURTURING PRACTICAL PHYSICALITY

Here are some ideas for helping your child value her physicality for how it lets her be in the world, rather than valuing it because of superficial external beauty or other blessings of chance.

DISCUSS CONCEPTS OF ATTRACTIVENESS

If you look with a critical eye at how real and imagined characters are presented in movies, books, and more, it is not hard to see that certain concepts of attractiveness are repeatedly put forth. As a parent, it is important to be aware of these images and have conversations with your child to emphasize that not everyone looks like those characters and neither would that be appropriate. Along those same lines, it is important to find role models in literature and film that look like your child so he sees himself represented.

Talk to your child about the fact that all people have strengths and weaknesses—mental, physical, and otherwise. The point here is not to teach your child that beauty or physical fitness are bad. The goal is to build your child's internal sense of value apart from external factors such as appearance.

As the late, great Fred Rogers once sang, "Everybody's fancy, everybody's fine." Help your child understand that physical differences between people are okay and to be appreciated for the variety they provide.

BE ACTIVE

I love walking in nature with my daughter. If you live in an urban area, it might be harder to find a nature path, but simply walking together around your neighborhood or in another safe, quiet place can achieve the same goal. Engaging in physical activities with your child is a way to model healthy movement as well as to get to know your child's preferences, capabilities, and interests better. It is a precious opportunity to connect.

As busy as most people are today, it can be hard to carve out time for walks like this, but it is possible. In some cultures, people walk after dinner instead of watching television. Even a ten-minute walk is a great way to develop a bond while being active.

Another low-stress idea for being physically active together is to have an at-home dance party. From the comfort of the living room and away from prying eyes, both parent and child can dance as crazy and silly as they want. Activities like this provide an opportunity to explore what is possible in terms of movement with one's body. In this safe, nonjudgmental space, try expressing yourselves by creating new dance moves with appropriately zany names. The focus here is for the child to have a deep experience of her body without fear of ridicule.

ENCOURAGE CURIOSITY

Approach this topic of physicality with curiosity. Help your child see new, appropriate physical endeavors as an opportunity to try on new ways of being.

When you suggest exploring positive physical endeavors to your kids, frame it from a place of curiosity: "Let's try it. You don't have to love it, but let's see what it's like."

If a child loves and appreciates the body and the role it plays in helping to achieve what she wants, she will take care of it. Here again, nurture curiosity. Encourage your child to find out what kind of healthy physical movement she enjoys and do more of it.

UNDERSTAND YOUR CHILD'S SELF-PERCEPTIONS

One of the recurring themes in this book is that it is important to truly know your child. One way to gain insight, particularly around the physical domain, is to set aside time for an art project, with the "assignment" being to draw a family portrait.

Art tends to be representational. Look at the child's depictions of relative sizes and the connections between people to facilitate a discussion. After the child is done drawing, you can ask questions from a place of curiosity, inquiring about expressions on people's faces as well as differences in size, clothing, and position. Your goal is not to correct. It is simply to understand. It is probably better for the parent not to draw during this activity because if the goal is to understand how your child is perceiving himself, you do not want to influence unduly what is drawn.

Drawing a family portrait is an especially effective activity for young children. When kids are older, you can be more direct about issues of physicality and self-perception. There are books and other kinds of media around which you can have a discussion about what they are thinking and observing around them.

Another way to understand your child's self-perceptions is to draw on the portrayal of people in movies and books. You could ask your child what he thinks of a certain character, heroes and villains alike, and how they are depicted.

A CAUTIONARY TALE

Parents should be aware of arming kids with skills that can be used against them. Starting at about age four, David took to karate like a duck to water. He loved it.

Then once while shopping in a clothing store, what was typical exploring behavior for a child his age became an amusing game of Catch Me If You Can. He used some of his newly learned karate skills to elude parents and salespeople as he cleverly and smoothly darted about the store. He slipped from aisle to aisle, using his ducking maneuver to free himself from a frustrated parent. Whew! We weren't expecting that.

My husband and I did join David for some of these karate lessons, which continued long enough to earn a black belt. Such physical activity gives the parents a chance to see the child in a different arena and also provides an opportunity to have the excellent guidance of the sensei.

As a preteen, David played soccer. That activity provided a space for him to not only learn and exercise team player skills, but to discover his team leadership ability as well. We saw an aspect of his personality that was somewhat new to us. He was efficiently aggressive, had a cold-steel determination to win, and was amazingly agile. As a young adult, he came to terms with the limitations of his own body. No matter how much he mentally subscribed to his favorite mantra—"Pain is weakness leaving the body"—the reality was that it was unlikely that he could play professionally.

WELL-BEING

Physical activity and fitness have benefits for building perseverance, discipline, and focus—all important in developing resiliency. Rather than viewing physical activity as an end in itself, parents should communicate the value of maintaining the body as a way to support overall mental and emotional well-being. Help children appreciate the body for how it lets them be in the world, not as their source of self-worth.

Just as the home can be a place to try on new physical endeavors, it can provide a safe place for children to learn and practice emotional resilience.

CHAPTER 5

Developing an Emotional Tool Kit

"The chief task in life is simply this: to identify and separate matters so that I can say clearly to myself which are externals not under my control, and which have to do with the choices I actually control. Where then do I look for good and evil? Not to uncontrollable externals, but within myself to the choices that are my own."

—EPICTETUS, DISCOURSES, 2.5.4–5

During a family video chat not long ago, my nieces showed Lena pictures from *Charlotte's Web*, the book they were reading with my sister. Lena was quite intrigued. I found a copy online and started reading it with her. She loved the story so much that I decided to look for the video version.

We were about a third of the way through the book at the time we watched the video. I had forgotten what happens at the end. Charlotte dies. Not only does she die, but she leaves behind her unborn babies. Charlotte's friend, Wilbur the pig, takes the egg sac filled with the little ones back to the farm and cares for them until they are born. Most of the tiny spiders strike out to find homes away from the farm, but a few remain. Wilbur tells them all about their remarkable mother, Charlotte, who was clever, compassionate, and above all, the best friend a lonely little pig could have.

When the movie ended, Lena asked, "Why does Charlotte die?"

My husband and I were caught off-guard. We were not prepared to have this discussion with our four-year-old, but we tried to explain as best we could.

"Well, are you going to die?" Lena asked. "Am I going to die? Are my friends going to die?" I struggled to answer her questions in a way that would be truthful and yet not overly frightening to her young mind.

A few days later we watched an old *Mister Rogers' Neighborhood* episode in which Mr. Rogers visits the local bakery. A folk singer, Andy Holiner, performs for an assemblage of children sitting all about him. Strumming his guitar, he gets them all singing "This Little Light of Mine." Before the song, he talks about the light being our life force and he looks the children squarely in their eyes and says of the light he sees there, "I can see it, right there in your eyes."

After we finished watching, Lena and I talked about the light in people's eyes and what it means to be alive. We continued this discussion when we walked in the forest near our home. We talked about the birds and beetles and squirrels we saw and what it means for them to be alive. At times, I felt utterly inadequate to the task of explaining, but I powered on, hoping that open dialogue would be the key to helping Lena understand.

In this chapter, we are going to discuss the importance of not shying away from tough discussions like these—even when you feel uncomfortable and maybe a bit unqualified to tackle them. Having tough conversations with trusted guardians is one way young children develop their emotional tool kit. They need to look squarely at potentially upsetting realities to learn how to process what they are seeing and respond in healthy ways. As parents, we can help them do so in a safe environment.

As with the other characteristics discussed thus far, each child has a different emotional makeup. Some will more readily share their feelings; others tend to hold emotions close to the vest. Some are naturally better at handling uncomfortable feelings, and some need extra help. As a parent, knowing your child's emotional traits will help you know how to foster resilience-encouraging behaviors.

CHILDREN NEED A SAFE ENVIRONMENT

Learning new emotional responses and trying on new behaviors is predicated on being in a safe, loving environment. We want to emphasize that if the environment is not safe for the child to express himself, then caution must be taken. For example, if one parent in the home has challenges around appropriate expression of emotions, like uncontrolled and disproportionate outbursts of anger, then it is probably not safe for children to test emotional boundaries. Allowing space for developing this tool kit is important, but it has to be with a trusted adult. Children tend to sense with whom they can share, but it can be good to reemphasize what spaces are safe.

A safe environment is loving, a place where parents approach their child's emotional growth in an open-hearted way. We acknowledge that this is no small feat. As any parent knows, children are natural-born masters at pushing boundaries and testing the proverbial waters of their parents' patience. This can be exhausting to navigate.

Another way that this idea of a safe space can manifest is in a personal haven, where the child can go when feeling upset or overwhelmed. On another recent extended family group call that included both adults and children, my uncle took the conversation into emotionally charged terrain. In response, my ten-year-old niece left the room and went to her safe place. She knows to go there when she needs a break. Her emotional tool kit has already been developed to the point where she has clear boundaries and can recognize, "I'm not comfortable anymore. I'm going to step away from this." Later, after reflecting, she was able to share her thoughts and feelings on the topic with my sister.

Though my daughter is much younger, she also has a safe place where she can go to think about whatever is upsetting her. Her spot includes special stuffed animals, activities, and other sources of comfort. Sometimes I go sit with her when she has retreated to this place, and sometimes, I am the one to suggest that she go there. Lena already knows that it is a safe space where she can express emotions without judgment and fear of punishment.

EMOTIONAL UPSET IS OKAY

According to an *Atlantic* article on parenting kids with anxiety, learning to endure emotional upset and distress is as

112 · RAISING GRITTY KIDS

important to long-term well-being as learning to tolerate physical pain.[23] Just as many parents try to shield their children from the smallest physical mishap, some try to guard against the emotional equivalent of a scraped knee. Understanding that it is okay for children to experience a certain amount of emotional upset can give parents freedom from the pressure always to swoop in and make things better. Children have to learn how to experience a bit of turmoil and navigate it on their own, without parental interference to smooth things over.

Many of the experts Kate Julian interviewed for the article also note the importance of addressing anxious tendencies early in life. Children who learn to manage anxiety early are more likely to be resilient to mental health challenges later in life. Conversely, children who do not develop the tools to handle anxiety are more likely to develop other mental health issues, or as Julian puts it, "friend disorders," over time.

It is important for children also to understand that experiencing joy and gratitude is as transient as sadness and anger. As much as we love feeling these more positive emotions, they do not last either. Help your child learn to cherish the positive experiences while also recognizing that they are impermanent. There might be great enjoyment in eating a scrumptious ice cream cone on a hot summer day, and then a feeling of disappointment when it is done. Alas, it is uncomfortable, but not forever.

ACCOMMODATING BEHAVIORS

According to the same article in the *Atlantic*, parents sometimes engage in accommodating behaviors in the name of expediency. However, these short-term fixes do not help children in the long run.

We get it. Most people today are very busy. The consequence of this is that opportunities for developing emotional resilience sometimes take a backseat to convenience. When you are rushing to get out the door, it can be excruciating to wait patiently as those tiny fingers fumble with shoe laces or jacket zippers. It can be so tempting to step in and offer some heroic assistance.

The examples are myriad; for instance, sparing the child the repercussions of not finishing homework by giving a little aid to help him complete it or making accommodations to get a picky eater to eat anything, anything at all. In the latter case, experts provide some concrete guidance here. Offer your child clear options, explaining the result of choosing none.

Choosing from a small set of appropriate options gives children a sense of agency and the experience of witnessing cause and effect in their own lives. Sure, it can be tough to sit by and watch as your child pairs the animal-print leggings with the floral dress and the neon rainboots, but in the grand scheme, it is far more empowering than harmful. And it is one small way you help your child build the understanding that one's choices shape one's life.

TYPICAL DEVELOPMENTAL STAGES

Certain emotions are connected with different stages of development. Parents might observe a certain reaction or behavior and come to the conclusion that this will be a fixed trait. When Lena was about a year old, she would go on great organizing sprees, sorting her toys and other objects by color, by size, by shape. My husband expressed some concern that we were witnessing the early stages of a more serious obsessive-compulsive disorder. A bit of research on my part assured him that this was a natural stage of development and we need not worry.

Another area of development that can be perplexing for new parents especially is what I call the "self-centered" stage. For a few months, it seemed that Lena could not get enough of her own reflection—in mirrors, in windows, even in the glossy front of the refrigerator. It can be helpful to understand that certain behaviors are common at a certain age.

Seeking out a bit of information online from reputable childhood development sources can help put your mind at ease about what constitutes normal behavior and what might be a flag for more attention. When parents have an understanding of typical emotional development, they can better help their child as well.

MEAN STREETS

"Who is in control of these mean streets?" This was the question that our four-year-old asked as he sat quietly in the back seat of our car. We had just left the Montessori school. He had been unusually quiet, and then suddenly the question came.

Early in the month, my son had lost the man who helped him learn to ride his bicycle, the man who had patiently guided him along the sidewalk, first with training wheels and then until he was steady enough to ride alone. He had lost his grandpa, and he was asking why bad things happen to good people. He was mourning.

DEVELOPING AN EMOTIONAL TOOL KIT · 115

Adults may forget or fail to understand how profoundly some children experience loss. The intensity may not be the same for all children. For my son, it was significant. His preschool teacher shared with me the drawings he produced for a few days. He would start off with a nice picture and then use a black crayon to carefully cover it, as if wiping it out.

. . . .

TOOL KIT FOR NURTURING EMOTIONAL DEVELOPMENT

This is one area of development that will be constantly evolving as your child grows. As such, the ways in which you provide support will also shift over time. These are some tools you might use as you shepherd your child from the toddler stage through to young adulthood.

HIT PAUSE

When your child is having a strong emotional reaction, you must find a way to calm things down before attempting a conversation. Although I do not usually advocate for diversionary tactics, they can be valuable in a situation like this. Redirect the child's attention to something else temporarily to effect a pause in the meltdown.

If you do not mind being a bit dramatic yourself, another method is to emote with the child. My mom mentioned that at times she tried crying along with an inconsolable child, or growling like a tiger in mock anger with a frustrated one. Suddenly, surprised to see an adult acting so uncharacteristically, the child quiets and there is now enough space to comfort and address the problem.

116 · RAISING GRITTY KIDS

When Lena is angry, I might say something like, "I see how angry you are. Can you show me by stomping your feet? Let's stomp our feet together." I'll join her and we'll stomp from room to room. Then I might pause and say, "Can you stomp even harder? Can you stomp just your left foot? How about your right? Can you stomp your feet and clap your hands at the same time?" Soon her anger dissipates, sometimes to be replaced with laughter.

Hitting pause on really intense emotions can enable the child to move from a place of overwhelm to one where he can share constructively.

HAVE A CONVERSATION

Once the child is no longer in the throes of the intense emotion, stop and initiate a conversation: "What's going on? Why are you so angry?" In this way, the child's feelings are acknowledged and validated, she has been given a chance to explain, and it opens the way for exploring different options for moving forward.

Parents who identify as more strict may be inclined to address any "out-of-control" behavior with punishment. Instead, try having a conversation once the intense emotion has stopped. This provides an opportunity to teach emotional management skills and give your child positive tools to handle these uncomfortable feelings.

In the conversation phase you could try sharing, in the calmest tones you can muster, what I call a "Facts about Emotions" list. It goes like this:

DEVELOPING AN EMOTIONAL TOOL KIT · 117

- Everyone has feelings.
- Emotions come and go.
- We all move through them.
- It is empowering to know that emotions do not last, that this too shall pass.
- We have a certain amount of control over our emotions. You do too.

Help your child understand that emotional upset will happen. Sometimes she will feel uncomfortable. Sometimes she will experience intense emotions. These feelings will happen, but they will pass.

READY, SET, COUNTDOWN TO ONE

If a child is upset—even a child of three or four—she can be given space to explain her reaction. Rather than dismiss her as too young or unable to understand a situation, give the child a chance to vocalize what is going on from her perspective. In so doing, you validate the child's emotional response underneath the outward reaction, not the outburst itself.

After you hear what the child is feeling, guide her in finding a better way to express it. For example, if your child is angry, help her try on a new behavior when angry—instead of acting out or yelling, your child could practice taking slow, deep breaths and counting from five to one before she speaks.

SET BOUNDARIES

Bullying is a big concern for many parents, especially as children enter elementary and middle school. One of the ways to help your child handle bullying behavior is to help her develop strong boundaries and have a pathway for open communication with you. The stronger a child's boundaries, the harder it is for a bully to get traction. But of course, some situations require the intervention of a trusted adult to resolve.

Another popular notion today is that people should have a positive emotional landscape, and that it is important for children to develop empathy and compassion. This is true. However, children also need to have boundaries. They need to know what they will tolerate, what is important to them, and what they will not stand for. Encourage your child to think about these things and share them with you.

It is a somewhat sophisticated discussion to have, but quite important. For example, a child might take a stand against a classmate who says mean, hurtful things while simultaneously having a feeling of compassion for the aggressor. Lena had a situation like this with a boy in her class who was teasing her. We role-played different ways she could respond, such as putting her hands on her hips and saying, "I don't like that." At the same time, I wanted to help Lena see that it was okay to not like what this boy was doing, but without labeling him a bad boy.

Knowing what one values provides a foundation to stand strong in the face of dissenting opinion and to take action to right wrongs. This powerful combination will serve your child well long into the future.

IDENTIFY ACCOMMODATING BEHAVIORS

Do a little self-assessment. Where are you accommodating? Where are you protecting your child from uncomfortable situations? In what areas are you choosing the short-term gain without thinking about whether that decision is helping your child in the long run?

If you have identified any areas that seem to apply, come up with a plan for how to respond differently. In the moment, it can be very hard to do things differently. Making a plan can serve you well.

Earlier, we shared the recommendation from the *Atlantic* article on how to handle accommodating behaviors. In other areas where these behaviors crop up, think about new actions you could take. For example, allowing a young child to select clothes from a few options the night before can make getting dressed in the morning less of a battle.

Here are some other common areas where parents might make accommodations, or smooth things over to help the child avoid uncomfortable emotions or because it is just easier and less exhausting to give in:

- Elaborate bedtime rituals (for example, meeting demands that all the stuffies be situated in a precise manner, that the blankets be arranged in a particular way, that a preset collection of songs and stories must be covered, etc.)
- Past a certain age, being consistently unable to sleep alone
- Homework and other areas where the child should be taking responsibility
- Reversing direction on things like sweets and screen time because the child's pleas are too much to take
- Bribing the child (with food, toys, privileges, etc.) to get the desired behavior in the moment

Chances are, when you first address accommodating behaviors, you could be in store for emotional tumult, both yours and your child's. Have a plan for how to respond. Both parents should be on board with this response and it should be applied consistently. If you and your partner are not on the same page, your child may pick up on that and potentially exploit it.

SET EXPECTATIONS

As stated in chapter 2, authoritative parenting, which has been shown in longitudinal studies to be the most effecting style, is marked by a balance of demandingness and responsiveness. Demandingness, in particular, involves setting clear expectations and then enforcing them.

For example, it is perfectly acceptable to expect your child to display calm behavior in public places, rather than screaming and running wild. Encourage calm, quiet, centered behavior, even in young children. If children know what behavior is expected, they will rise to the occasion. Everyone does better when they know what is expected.

Expectations can be set lovingly, which is important. You do not want to label the behavior you are steering away from as wrong, per se. Better to encourage children to act in a different way.

My daughter is incredibly high energy. From morning to night, she is on the go. Sometimes when we have settled down for a weekend afternoon story, Lena continues to wriggle and get distracted. When this happens, I pause, give her a hug, and say, "Okay, let's count to five and then we'll go back to reading." My tone of voice is key. I do not want to communicate that her energy level or movement is wrong. I simply want to lovingly redirect her to a different, more appropriate frame of mind for the current activity.

DEVELOP A CHORE CALENDAR

Create a chore calendar that clearly spells out tasks your child is expected to complete each day or week. Even children three or four years old can follow a chore calendar if they are shown how. Julie Lythcott-Haims, former Dean of Freshman at Stanford, cites the Harvard Grant Study, one of the longest-running continuous studies of adult development. She says, "[The study finds] that professional success in life...comes from having done chores as a kid. And the earlier you start it, the better."[24]

Chore calendars help children develop a sense of responsibility, and perhaps just as importantly, they provide good training ground for parents. Almost certainly, you can complete each task in much less time, so it will take patience for you to stand back and let the child do it.

Emotionally speaking, completing chores can provide a sense of accomplishment. However, each individual task can be frustrating, especially for young children who have not completed the activity before. As the parent, you are helping them move through the frustration and hang with it through to completion—a valuable tool in the resiliency tool kit.

Frustration is an important emotion to identify and then work with constructively. In the country where I live, most families have washing machines but no clothes dryers. As a result, we

122 · RAISING GRITTY KIDS

hang our clothes on a drying rack with clothespins. One day, my daughter wanted to help hang up the clothes. She found it challenging and became frustrated. Finally, Lena said, "I'm not doing this!"

"Okay," I replied. "Let's take a break and come back to it."

When we came back, I said, "Let me show you how I do it." It was important for her to experience working through the frustration and figuring out the steps of how to accomplish the task. By the end, she was hanging her socks and leggings on her own and felt so pleased.

As described earlier, it is important to hit pause when a child drifts toward overwhelm—pause, not quit. After the child calms down some, provide guidance so she can complete the task on her own. Learning to power through frustrating or challenging activities is a great way to build resilience.

To communicate that completing chores and working around the house are family activities, you might consider not paying an allowance to perform them. From a 2018 *Atlantic* article comes insight from Heather Beth Johnson, a sociologist at Lehigh University. "When we pay [kids] to do things that humans have always had to do as participants of communities and families…it sends them some sort of a message that they are entitled to [an] exchange for these things, as opposed to a message that they're part of a household team and should contribute accordingly."[25]

David Lancy of Utah State University suggests that parents start the practice of assigning chores as early as eighteen months.[26] In an earlier interview, he said, "Toddlers are very eager to be helpful...in fact, I think we are doing a disservice to toddlers and older children when we deny them the opportunity to pitch in and be helpful."[27]

As mentioned, it can be hard to let children help at a young age because it is not the most efficient. However, if you shut them down when they want to help, they will learn to stop volunteering their services.

One thing to be aware of as you create a chore calendar is the equity of the tasks assigned to girls and boys. Studies have shown that the housework distribution is not always equitable, nor is the typical allowance paid for doing these chores. Giving any allowance is a personal choice, but if you do, be thoughtful about the compensation you are giving sons and daughters and the message you are sending.

I REMEMBER MAMA

Cleanliness is next to godliness. That rule was part of the overarching tapestry of cultural values when I grew up. After all, if Jesus came to your house, you'd want it to be sparkling clean from corner to corner. In parts of Europe in the eighteenth or nineteenth century, it was the king that people in the villages might expect as a visitor. Keeping the hut tidy was a priority.

Mama loved a clean, well-organized house. Some people could hire others to do the work of house cleaning, shoe shining, car washing, and whatever else was deemed necessary. She couldn't afford to hire, and so she did it herself until we were old enough to help.

Mama married young, and by the time she was about thirty, she had

124 · RAISING GRITTY KIDS

five children, as was typical at the time. The three oldest were assigned jobs as soon as they were old enough to learn how to perform them thoroughly.

Each Saturday was general cleaning day. Chores were rotated. Dish washing was the most fun. What kid doesn't like putting his hands in clean, warm, sudsy water? Plus, you could take your time. Sweeping and dusting was the most coveted assignment because the task could be completed quickly. Floors throughout the bungalow were to be swept, scatter rugs removed and shaken out, and the floor underneath swept before replacing them. When you saw the result, you were left with a feeling of satisfaction at a job well done.

For me, the least desirable job was ironing. Back in the day, every home had an iron and an ironing board, which were used regularly as the wash and wear-type of fabrics did not exist or at least weren't available to most. My oldest sister loved ironing. The "cat faces" were a problem for me, tiny creases in the fabric that would appear seemingly out of nowhere when ironing. It could be very frustrating because the more you tried to get them out, the worse things started to get.

Years later, I came to understand that my reaction possibly came from a perfectionist trait that tended to run in the family. As a teenager when we were living in Chicago and Mama was going to work every day, she hired a member of our church to do the ironing. This lady was an expert at the craft of pressing shirts, suit coats, and any complex garment. She showed me the secret to avoiding cat faces, and with that, my dread of ironing disappeared.

One day, my brother decided to take a shortcut on the sweeping and dusting. We had frittered away housecleaning time playing and inventing new games. It was almost time for our parents to return from work. Upon hearing Dad enter the house, he quickly placed the scatter rug in our bedroom, over what he had swept.

DEVELOPING AN EMOTIONAL TOOL KIT · 125

Dad entered the room to see if chores had been done. We watched anxiously as he checked to see if furniture had been dusted, and we thought we were in the clear when he turned to leave the room. But, he didn't. Instead he stopped. Noticing a bump in the rug, he carefully lifted one corner of it and revealed the source of our fear. He was angry and removed his belt, stood in the doorway, and insisted that the job be properly done, which involved at least three trips past him with the belt at the ready to inflict a reminder that we were not to let this happen again. In those days, corporal punishment was not an unusual parenting strategy.

● ●

PROVIDE DAILY FREE TIME

Get into the habit of giving your child a set amount of free time to do whatever he or she wants. Whether it is five minutes or fifteen, make sure to provide this time every day.

During this free time, you should be present and interacting with your child, but not telling or directing the activity. This is an uninterrupted chance for the child to be director of his world. This strengthens the sense of autonomy, self-direction, and provides ample opportunity for the child to see cause-effect relationships unfold that do not involve the parent.

READ BOOKS WITH LESSONS AND ASK QUESTIONS

Look online for a list of books that teach lessons related to emotions: being angry, being different, forgiving, bullying, losing a grandparent, losing a pet, and more real-life, potentially uncomfortable situations. Reading and discussing these books with your child provides an entry point to have a dialogue about thornier topics.

126 · RAISING GRITTY KIDS

Along those lines, *Mister Rogers' Neighborhood* remains a wonderful and well-conceived resource to introduce difficult topics. Fred Rogers was a towering giant of child advocacy, sparking a cultural revolution in how we speak and interact with and nurture children. Check out the many beloved songs and episodes at www.misterrogers.org.

MEDITATE

Helping children develop their emotional tool kit can be quite exhausting for parents too. I have found that a regular meditation practice has helped me develop more patience in all areas of life. You can include your children in a shorter version of your practice. Three minutes is probably a good starting place for young children. When Lena joins me, she will sit on my lap for a few minutes of connection, stillness, and quiet.

If you are interested but unsure where to start, try googling "meditation for parents" and "meditation for children." There are also many meditation apps that can launch you on your journey.

Some people shy away from meditation because they believe it is not congruent with their spiritual practices. Depending on the style of meditation you adopt, it can be compatible with any spiritual practices you already have. At its core, it is about developing awareness of the disquiet in mind to more readily find and tap into the internal quiet place that does exist for us all.

READ PARENTING ARTICLES

Read the *Atlantic* article referenced earlier, titled "Childhood in an Anxious Age" in the print version and "What Happened to American Childhood?" online. Look for other articles that address specific emotional issues like anger, bullying, and age-appropriate development.

GET HELP IF NEEDED

If you recognize that your child is experiencing extreme emotional upheaval—depression, debilitating anxiety, anger that leads to self-harm or harm to others—find professional assistance. It might also help to read articles on the area of concern to know that you are not the only parent seeing these things in a child. However, for more serious issues, it is important to get help from a trusted source to chart the best path forward.

HANDLING DIFFICULT EMOTIONS

The emotional component of resiliency used to be a more gendered discussion where certain emotions were acceptable for different genders. Today, however, it is understood that a full and healthy range of emotions is key for resiliency for both boys and girls.

Helping your child develop skills to handle emotions effectively will pay dividends well into the future. It helps to start introducing these lessons gradually. Children who know how to sit with uncomfortable emotions and persevere in the face of challenges grow to be more resilient and tend to launch more successfully when it is time to go out on their own.

Next, we will look at the social component of your child, along with the shifting social landscape.

CHAPTER 6

Developing Social Presence in a Shifting Landscape

"Education is the best weapon for peace."
—MARIA MONTESSORI, *EDUCATION AND PEACE*

The Christmas when Lena was three, she received a train set. She absolutely loved it and had great fun putting it together, manipulating the switches, turning on the lights, and changing the direction of the trains by way of tiles on the tracks. She wanted to show her gift to my mother-in-law and grandmother-in-law, so we brought the set to their house one day. Lena put the tracks together and then demonstrated everything her beloved train could do. My grandmother-in-law looked at Lena and asked somewhat incredulously, "What is this? Are you a little boy?"

Lena's great-grandmother came of age during World War II, a very different time. She was a dedicated housewife who cooked, looked after the children, and sewed all their clothes.

On more than one occasion, she has given me advice about how to dress, what type of shoes to wear, and even how to enter a room for maximum impact. She is very strong in her own right, and she has strong ideas about femininity and proper behavior for a little girl. That she found it odd that I endorsed Lena's love of the train set highlights the ways in which her perspective is very different from my own. It is much more acceptable today for all children to play with toys that in the past may have been more typical for one gender or the other. It is merely one manifestation of a more general shift in thinking, in this case around gender roles specifically.

Parents cannot always predict what the future will look like, but the goal is to raise children who are flexible and adaptable, who can change with the times, rather than be stuck in one set way of thinking about societal roles. All individuals can exert a certain amount of control over their own ideas about who they are and how they show up in the world. However, the reality is that as one circulates and functions within the larger community, the collective perspective can be more challenging to navigate and transcend. Our aim in this chapter is to discuss ways to prepare your child to traverse the inevitable shifts in the social landscape, while remaining true to personal preferences, choices, and values.

IT'S NOT YOUR GRANDDAD'S WORLD

The world is changing in profound ways. There is no way around that. To name just a few of the fronts along which change is happening: demographic shifts in America's age and ethnic composition, the ongoing evolution of our understanding of gender and gendered roles, an increased interest in personal development and self-actualization, consideration of what constitutes community and the ways in which technology helps or hinders how we connect and interact, a reexamination of privacy and personal freedoms, and deep debates about how to grow sustainably and equitably. Standing amidst all of this could feel disconcerting for anyone. Parents have the added responsibility of looking out over it all and trying to make the choices that will best enable their child to thrive no matter how the future ultimately looks.

To help your child develop the resilience that will be key to navigating the future, we recommend nurturing three primary characteristics—curiosity, tolerance, and flexibility. The challenge is to encourage children to develop a personal compass, while maintaining curiosity about other people's choices and the tolerance to let others do what works for them. This balancing act requires some flexibility of mind but in the long run can help children face and overcome the many interpersonal issues they may face. We are not saying that parents must fully embrace every social change in their landscape, nor must their children, but tolerance for others helps make the world livable for all. That is our aim.

Community, society, and culture sometimes signal disapproval of certain expressions of individuality, especially when they do not conform with accepted norms. If your child happens to be a maverick, someone who falls outside the spectrum of generally accepted societal norms, it is important to nurture individuality while also being honest about the possible consequences of full expression. Plenty of people in the world do not embrace the curiosity and tolerance that would allow space for nonjudgment of others' fully expressed and unique lifestyles.

It is worth noting that one key benefit of living in a democratic society is that there still exists a degree of freedom of movement and choice. If your current tribe is not working for you, it is possible to strike out and find a community, or even construct one, that might be more suitable. Of course, this is easier said than done, and it requires a certain type of courage to pursue, but it can provide hope to those who feel like outsiders in their current circumstances. Remember the crocodile, who for the benefit of its offspring surveys the landscape and makes adjustments as required.

A FEW THOUGHTS ON GENDER

Whereas my husband's grandmother and my paternal grandmother stayed at home, cooked, sewed, and cared for the children almost exclusively, Lena is seeing different behaviors modeled. All around her, she sees examples of women not only working outside the home, but sometimes being the primary breadwinner. One time before she could even read or write, Lena asked if she could have a toy laptop and phone so she could work alongside me. "Oh, Mama. I'm going to help you on your calls!" She was excited to get to work.

Society still has certain dictates around behavior that is acceptable for one gender but not the other. I remain on guard for how my own limiting conceptions might be creeping into my language or expectations for Lena. When she went through a particularly assertive phase at around two and a half, I was careful not to label her behavior as bossy. Are little boys *ever* described as bossy? Rarely. It is a loaded term usually used to describe girls who tell other people what to do.

Frankly, I want Lena to embrace her budding leadership skills, not be shamed for them. Whenever the "bossy" label comes

132 · RAISING GRITTY KIDS

up, I do two things. First, I try to provide Lena with more discrete opportunities to exert control over her world. Second, when someone unthinkingly uses that term, I try to reframe it as Lena taking charge of the situation and her choices.

Have my conversations with others shifted the landscape Lena will one day traverse? It is too early to know if something as small as this will have an impact. Regardless, it has certainly led to many interesting discussions with friends, family, and even strangers about how we can all encourage more positive conceptions of female leadership from day one.

Along similar lines, there remain norms around what emotions are appropriate, especially for boys. Learning to process and express feelings in appropriate ways is a hallmark of emotional maturity, and it is critical for resiliency. Although notions around what is acceptable have shifted quite a lot from even one generation ago, parents still need to be aware of the language they use and the unspoken signals of disapproval they may be sending to the child.

IMPORTANCE OF EXPOSURE

One of the main goals of this book is to guide parents in helping their children develop a tool kit for navigating uncertain terrain. We advocate for giving children a safe place to try out new behaviors while they are young so that they have had lots of practice by the time they launch out on their own. In a way that is age-sensitive, you can gradually expose your child to the complexities of living within a vibrant society comprising individuals with varied viewpoints, preferences, and values. By not shielding them from difficult discussions on emotionally charged or controversial topics, you ensure that they have a safe place to ask questions and explore ways to respond constructively to the challenges they may face.

The reality is that your children will meet people who do not like or approve of them, simply because of how they look or the lifestyle they are living. The sooner they have tools to handle the negativity that may be headed their way, the better.

Coming to understand that others do not always wish you well is a necessary, if painful, rite of passage. Accepting that truth does not make it any easier to watch as your child's innocence is stripped away, sometimes in an instant.

When my daughter was a preschooler, I experienced a stark reminder of how even I, who remain ever vigilant, cannot always protect Lena from the hurt others may direct her way. On Lena's first trip to a world-class and historic city, she was giddy with excitement everywhere we went. She loved the new foods we were trying and all the pretty, sparkly objects we observed in shop windows as we walked to nearby landmarks. She marveled at the strange language everyone around us was speaking, her first experience immersed in something other than the two we speak at home.

We made a trip to the classic amusement park, the one where all the locals go, and were happily making our way to a special magic show. Out of nowhere, a young boy jumped into our path, mimicking a monkey, and attempted to knock us off our feet.

In another situation, even more upsetting, a little girl came up to Lena and spat on her. Why this hostile reception? Truthfully, I can only guess. After tears and much consternation,

134 · RAISING GRITTY KIDS

Lena and I talked about what had happened and what it might mean. We talked about how people's actions can hurt, but we also talked about the nice people we had met on our trip. Needless to say, Lena's open-hearted enthusiasm for this place had been greatly diminished. As we returned to the airport a couple of days later, she remarked that she was glad to be heading home where people loved and cared for her.

ENCOURAGING TOLERANCE

There are many ways to expose your child gradually and consistently to diverse people and situations. You can read books that feature families that do not look like your own. You can talk about social issues in the news (at an age-appropriate level, of course). You can travel to different areas of the country as well as abroad.

On the one hand, you want your child to feel comfortable in his own skin—even if that does not fit the "norm" of his family, school, or neighborhood. You want him to know that he is okay, and that even though there might be hardships along the way, you are there to help him. At the same time, you want to help your kids learn how to respect and honor other people's humanity.

Just as with the other facets of character, the natural inclination toward tolerance or judgment varies by child. Some are more naturally outgoing and willing to connect with others who are different. Some are more introspective and might prefer learning about others' perspectives in more indirect ways, like reading or watching movies or hearing stories from others.

The unknown can be scary for anyone, but especially for

DEVELOPING SOCIAL PRESENCE IN A SHIFTING LANDSCAPE · 135

children. The antidote is exposure to different landscapes: racial, cultural, familial, and otherwise. The reason is twofold. First, in being known, difference becomes less scary. Second, through exposure and with your guidance, your child will learn how to better discern which situations are different but okay, versus those that are simply unsafe or unsavory for other reasons.

Sometimes it may feel like social constructs are set in stone and that change comes about slowly, if at all. In reality, social shifts can happen rapidly, faster than one might have anticipated. By nature of your parenting choices, you are shaping the world we all inhabit. If every parent took a stand for tolerance and curiosity, the world would look very different indeed.

You may be familiar with the saying "Sticks and stones will break my bones, but words will never harm me." This folk wisdom has been around a long time, with the earliest documented citation coming from March 1862 in the *Christian Recorder*, the weekly periodical of the African Methodist Episcopal Church.[28] The truth is that words, as much as actions, do have the power to shape the world in which one lives. And so, it is vitally important to be thoughtful and deliberate in both, particularly because the child models what he observes as acceptable in his limited social setting and brings those conceptions with him as he grows older and his social sphere expands.

The *Christian Recorder* goes on to say, "True courage consists in doing what is right, despite the jeers and sneers of our companions." It seems the original meaning was deeper than merely encouraging one to brush off the insults of those who mean ill. And herein lies the challenge—to be at once strong,

136 · RAISING GRITTY KIDS

single-minded, compassionate, and well-balanced. The child who grows into these characteristics will be well equipped to navigate most anything.

AMERICA THE DIVERSE

This is a tough one. How to describe this complex landscape that we've inherited? How to share thoughts on a topic when you're still learning? Many discussions with friends and family members have helped shape my ideas. The following represents my point of view for now, which to be honest, may change. And that's okay.

The country itself is a work in progress. In 1788, Alexander Hamilton is said to have used the term "grand experiment," and indeed, the experiment continues. There remains a lot to learn about the diversity that existed on the continent of North America before our ancestors arrived.

As youngsters, we were required to memorize Emma Lazarus's lofty words, which are inscribed on the base of the Statue of Liberty and welcomed long-ago immigrants to their new country. We could easily recite, "Give me your tired, your poor..." We were taught that statues and monuments were enduring structures, weighty in their meaning and symbolism.

Many have forgotten, or perhaps never knew, that the champion of the statue was Edouard Laboulaye, the Frenchman who helped design it and gave it the name "Liberty Enlightening the World." He hoped it would commemorate the end to slavery in America. Recently freed slaves gave of their meager, hard-earned funds to help purchase the pedestal on which Lady Liberty stands. Ironically, by the time the statue was erected, the landscape had shifted. Jim Crow laws, designed to reverse the celebrated gains, were firmly in place.

DEVELOPING SOCIAL PRESENCE IN A SHIFTING LANDSCAPE · 137

We are a complex nation of the indigenous as well as the hyphenated: Irish-Americans, Italian-Americans, African-Americans, and so on. Although some immigrants changed their names to become more "mainstream," they held onto certain traditions. One friend, who has Italian ancestors, has visited Italy more than once and knows something of its history. Some children of immigrants can still speak the language of their heritage. Most know their family narratives prior to coming to America. Admittedly, for one group in this country, there has been a profound and deliberate disconnect from family roots.

In the not-too-distant past, many African-Americans knew as much about Africa as any other American, which was often very little. Until recently, many thought the huge continent of Africa was a country. Some could name Egypt as a country, but were pretty sure it was close to, but not actually in Africa. A few could name Ethiopia.

Back in the day, what many Americans knew about the African continent was derived from movies like *Tarzan*. Many actually believed that all Africans spoke the Hollywood lingo heard in movies and had no idea that as many as two thousand well-documented African languages exist.

Why share this? In 1977, the public was introduced to Kunta Kinte. The TV miniseries based on the novel *Roots* captured the hearts and imaginations of over one hundred million Americans. It energized much talk about the need to correct the national ignorance and inadequate knowledge of history and geography. The thought emerged that it was unreasonable to consider oneself truly educated and at the same time know very little about one of the world's largest landmasses. Among baby boomers, there was also an increasing awareness of the elements of social injustice that contributed to a peculiar and oblique learning deficit that made ignorance both possible as well as persistent. Articles and books were written to inform and instruct. Today we know much more, and we're still learning.

138 · RAISING GRITTY KIDS

Clearly, our country is one accustomed to change. It is a place that has tried to accommodate ethnic, racial, political, and religious diversity. This was not always viewed as universally accomplished. In his autobiography, W. E. B. DuBois, historian and author of *The Souls of Black Folk*, spoke of the African-American perspective with a nuanced view of freedom and liberty.

It is true that some have come looking for greater opportunities. Some are escaping persecution, and some just want to begin again. Each in turn has become a part of the American experiment, which is all about being better, carving out a place, a new landscape that is better than what was left behind.

So, now what? While seeking to understand these shifts, we can say that all, for better or worse, have helped build America. Some, with their well-developed cultures, were already here. Others arrived and brought with them well-honed skills that had been practiced over decades, even centuries, in a previous homeland. They may have been the sons or daughters of tailors, bakers, bankers, engineers, brick masons, blacksmiths, boat builders, farmers, or planters of rice, tobacco, or cotton.

Interestingly, in his 1840 critique of American democracy, Alexis de Tocqueville noted that "Without common ideas, there is no common action, and without common action men still exist, but a social body does not. Thus, in order that there be society, and all the more, that this society prosper, it is necessary that all the minds of the citizens always be brought together and held together by some principle ideas."[29]

And so, we come to one principle idea of America. It is unique in its diversity, and diversity has helped to build this unique country, enviable in its gifts and successes. Now it is time for that diversity to help heal the fractures that exist.

Perhaps an analogy could be useful. Is it possible that a significant percentage of the population harbors some vague, unresolved grief? Not fully understanding the history, not knowing the past, has resulted in a kind of national "baggage." Yet the nation has done what individuals do when trying simply to survive: put one foot in front of the other and keep moving, preferably in a positive direction. But how to move forward more sustainably? What comes to mind is a program called The Grief Recovery Method by John James and Russell Friedman. Its purpose is to offer meaningful strategies for acknowledging and coping with loss. What applies for the individual may very well apply to the country at large.

The reality is that there is enough unexpressed hurt to go around. It has been said that unresolved pain might eventually implode. In one of his poems, Langston Hughes asks, "What happens to a dream deferred? Does it dry up like a raisin in the sun...Maybe it just sags like a heavy load. *Or does it explode?*"[30]

Without a doubt, the past influences the future. The cultural wellness of the country as a whole is intertwined in those words welcoming newcomers and acknowledging their pain. Are we the wretched, tempest-tost ones? There is no group that can claim a monopoly on trauma. All have experienced being a victim. All have been the victimizer.

It is entirely possible that the citizens of today will succeed in carving out an emotionally and spiritually healthy America. It seems that as a country, we are finally prepared to acknowledge that seemingly heroic accomplishments, built where a whirlwind of unresolved hurt and pain percolates subtly threatening to derail it all, constitute mere Pyrrhic victories.

How sad it is when building or owning the tallest building, having a garage with the fastest cars, earning several Pulitzers or Oscars, owning a coveted athletic franchise, building a rocket ship, discovering new creatures in the depths of the ocean, or creating a thrilling video game,

140 · RAISING GRITTY KIDS

does not bring lasting satisfaction and joy. Paulo Coelho says, "It is not winning or losing a single battle that matters, but how the war ends."[31]

We know that you cannot just say, "Love thy neighbor" when all around there's unresolved emotional injury. It is challenging, but we must confront the historical pain that unites us. For example, in this country, it is entirely conceivable that in the due course of genuine friendship, someone could struggle with how to tell an African-American colleague that a beloved great-grandfather was a valiant Confederate soldier, admired by the family for his courage, yet fighting to uphold the institution of slavery.

If there is to be positive change, there must be a time and a place to remember. Not to blame, but to reflect so that more informed decisions can be made in the future. Being actively involved in times of change may be necessary in order to understand and help shape the landscape. The bottom line is that we must make the effort to recognize the fallacies of old philosophies, while not discarding the strengths on which this country was built.

What are we? From where did we come? Where are we going? Despite moments of uncertainty, we can answer. We are a diverse people. Together we've come a long way and it has taken grit to do so. With a realistic knowledge of the shifting landscape, we are able to nurture resilience.

• •

TOOL KIT FOR DEVELOPING SOCIAL PRESENCE

This section provides tips to help your child foster curiosity, learn about others, and adjust to shifting social dynamics in today's world.

A PATH TO EMPATHY

As discussed earlier, exposure makes difference less scary. Learn about different cities, states, and countries, different cultures, races, traditions, families, foods, clothing, ideas, beliefs, and languages. Do this often.

As you introduce your child to the ways in which people live differently, start a conversation about what it might be like. How do their preferences and choices differ from the child's? What benefits and difficulties might others face? This is primarily an early exercise in empathy building, so the emphasis is on trying to understand rather than rushing to label or judge.

Books and music are a great way to introduce children to different families, lifestyles, cultures, races, and more. Try tailoring the reading material or music to the child's interests. For example, if your child loves the guitar, you could learn about a guitarist who grew up in a different state or country or plays a different style of music from what your child usually hears.

LISTEN FOR REFLEXIVE APOLOGIES

From a young age, girls more than boys are encouraged to say "sorry," to take on the emotional responsibility of apologizing and smoothing things over. The result can be too much automatic or reflexive apologizing even as they grow older. We are by no means saying that unpleasant, rude, or hurtful behavior should be tolerated. That is not the point. However, by getting into the habit of over-apologizing, the meaning and value of any apology may be diminished.

A way to talk to your daughter (or son, if the situation fits) about reflexive apologizing is to share the importance of reserving apologizing for situations where it is truly merited. There have been times where I apologized to my daughter. It is rare, but when I do, I am modeling situations where apologizing is appropriate, where I have reflected on what happened and realized that an apology is in order. I hope that this act also shows my daughter that I respect her as a person, albeit a small one. When I observe Lena reflexively apologizing to smooth things over in some situation, I take the time to help her see why an apology may not be necessary. I want her to be thoughtful about the words "I'm sorry."

As a parent, you have to be on your toes perpetually to listen for and seize opportunities to have meaningful conversations with your child. Hearing your child apologize is one opening for deeper connection around a situation. If an apology was warranted, you can have a conversation about what happened and why it might have been hurtful to another. If it is a reflexive apology, however, it may be an opportunity to help him come up with a more appropriate response.

TAKE ADVANTAGE OF TECHNOLOGY

Technology can be your aid in facilitating exploration of the world all around. Many world-class museums and galleries have excellent online offerings, some with options tailored specifically for children. Study languages, even if it is a few words or simple songs. Watch documentaries.

One small warning here: technology can be a double-edged sword in that it potentially opens the door to things you would not want your child exposed to. Besides the obvious examples of violent or graphic content, unwanted messaging can take many more subtle forms. For example, are girls being portrayed in a way that is unaligned with your values? Are other races or ethnicities being subtly denigrated? Are boys who display strong emotion portrayed as less than? Although potentially time consuming, it can be helpful in the long run to vet the websites your child visits so you know what is on offer.

My husband grew up in central Europe and wanted to share with Lena the cartoons he watched as a child. I was a little nervous at first because I knew the questionable nature of many cartoons I grew up watching in America. Several portrayed outdated gender roles and sometimes downright racist stereotypes. Needless to say, I watched a bunch of these old-school European cartoons before Lena did and found them to be quite charming.

EMBRACE GLOBAL INTERCONNECTEDNESS

Revisit some of your reflections from chapter 1. Consider how the nation and world might be in twenty-five years. This is the world your child will inhabit. While technology has removed many barriers to global interconnectedness, there are other forces moving in the opposite direction. How will this play out? Will communities and neighborhoods be different? What impact will climate change have? What social skills should your children develop now that will help them cope with new uncertainties? What are jobs going to look like? Will they need to know other languages in order to be competitive?

The answers to these questions are personal and unique. They also have real ramifications for the choices you make today as a parent. It is worthwhile to spend time thinking about the potential future social landscape as a way to inform and guide your current decisions.

As a young teen, I had a pen pal who lived in Senegal. I would send letters in my broken schoolgirl French, and he would respond graciously in his perfect French, sharing details about his day-to-day life in Dakar. I absolutely loved receiving those missives, the thin envelope paper covered in international air mail stamps.

I have embarked on a similar project with Lena. I found a charity that pairs a family with a child in a different country. There was a little boy, born the same day as Lena, with similarly bright and innocent eyes, and I knew he was the one we would sponsor. Now we send letters, and pictures of the funny squirrels who live in our backyard, and small birthday and Christmas gifts in addition to regular support for school fees and supplies. Lena has already asked if we can go visit Emmanuel one day, and I am hopeful that we will be able to do just that.

BE COURAGEOUS IN YOUR COMPASSION

From a young age, we are taught to love our neighbor. In a diverse society such as America, this is actually a supremely courageous act, and we need to recognize it as such. Carrying that hypothetical compassion through to real-life situations and encounters is sometimes hard to do. It takes courage to be curious, flexible, and tolerant. It can be difficult. It can be messy. However, the path to resiliency involves moving through ever-more challenging experiences and coming out stronger on the other side. There is no shortcut.

CHANGE IS INEVITABLE

None of us has a crystal ball about what the future holds. The only certainty is that change is inevitable. As a parent, the aim is not to prepare children for any particular future. Rather it is to prepare them for change itself. When you arm your child with tools to navigate whatever the future holds, it matters less how that future ultimately looks.

Whether you accept it or not, you are a major role model for your child. Own it and ask yourself frequently if what your child is observing is what you want to communicate. For parents, too, it is never too late to learn and exercise curiosity, flexibility, and tolerance.

On to the fifth facet of your child's makeup: spirituality.

CHAPTER 7

Nurturing Spirituality and Ethical Behavior

"Spiritual powers are a form of wealth. They must go into circulation so that others can enjoy them: they must be expressed, utilized, to complete the cycle of human relations."
—MARIA MONTESSORI, THE ABSORBENT MIND

When I was in the second grade, our class watched a video about Native Americans and how various tribes were pushed from their territories and forced to live on reservations. It was so long ago that I cannot remember most of the details of what we watched, but I do remember how profoundly sad I felt for days and weeks after. The video showed how people, whole families, succumbed to starvation, disease, and exposure during the journey. American frontiersmen and businessmen on pleasure hunts slaughtered the buffalo with a zealousness that was stoked from the knowledge that this act would further subjugate the tribes who relied on the animals for food, clothing, shelter, and religious rituals. Even to my seven-year-old mind, it seemed clear that there was little respect for the land, the animals, and the people.

Looking back, I am a little surprised at the depth of my reaction. The level of grief I felt was profound. I felt utterly distraught, almost in mourning for humanity at large. I remember not only empathizing with the Native Americans and buffalo but also feeling despair for the people who committed the acts that caused such suffering. It was depressing to understand that people could do such things to one another, and I wondered what the perpetrators must have been suffering themselves to inflict such cruelty on others.

That day is one of my earliest memories of being spiritually touched by something I saw. Although I probably would not have described it like this then, I believe it was the first time I felt a connection with all things—people, both victims and aggressors, animals, and the environment. My mom has noted that this was a portent of my ongoing interest in social equity and a desire to lead life from a place of love and compassion for all.

In this chapter, we will discuss the difference between spirituality and religion, the importance of nurturing spiritual growth according to each child's needs, and the connection between spirituality and ethics. As usual, we will close with tools for building your child's tool kit.

SPIRITUAL CURIOSITY

Of all the topics we have discussed so far, spirituality, with its inherently personal and inward focus, is the most complex. Each parent brings a distinct perspective to the equation, and partners are rarely on precisely the same page when it comes to spiritual questions. Add to the mix a child who is growing intellectually and emotionally in rapid bursts of curiosity, boundary-testing, and sense-making. Encompassing it all might be the broader family and community weighing in on what the parents and child should be thinking and feeling. Spirituality can be a minefield to navigate on many levels.

As such, I want to emphasize that there are many excellent books specific to different religious and spiritual beliefs. I encourage you to talk to spiritual advisors and counselors already in your life for guidance in broaching these topics with your child. Make use of resources that are specific to your cultural needs.

It would not be surprising to feel somewhat intimidated by this topic. The reasons are myriad. However, do not let intimidation impede you from engaging with your child about spiritual questions, if only on very practical grounds. Research shows that people who are more spiritually grounded have fewer substance abuse problems, tend to navigate depression better, and have better life outcomes—great reasons to brave any uncomfortable feelings that may come up in order to shepherd your child's spiritual growth.[32]

Allow your child to ask questions and engage in the exploration of these topics together. You do not need to have all the answers. More important than knowing what to say is being willing to have a conversation. Talk to your child about what he is thinking. Let him know it is okay to delve into tough questions about why things are the way they are. It is more than okay. It can be immensely meaningful in shaping the child's worldview and impacting life choices made well into the future.

RELIGION AND SPIRITUALITY

Whereas religion typically has a cultural aspect and is guided by dogma and rules, spirituality involves the feeling of being part of something much larger than oneself. It involves a sense of interconnectedness with all things that does not necessarily involve adherence to a specific set of rules or inclusion in particular rituals.

Ironically, by moving away from more organized religions, some are able to entertain discussions related to questions that might otherwise be off limits or considered heterodox. Remember that some of the greatest spiritual teachers in history began by moving through and challenging accepted thought.

Organized religion is just that—organized and planned, often offering a prescribed path to follow to salvation. Spirituality, on the other hand, is more of an individual journey inward to discover universal truths. Religion can be a path to spirituality—just as spirituality can be a path to religion—but it is not necessarily so. One can follow all the rules and rituals religiously, as it were, without truly embarking on the path to deeper spiritual understanding.

When I was confirmed at twelve in the mainline Protestant church we attended, there was great emphasis on the fact that this was a decision to be taken seriously. Our confirmation leaders emphasized that officially joining the congregation was our choice. For it to be an active choice, we were provided substantial exposure to other religions, with their traditions and rituals, so we truly understood the implications of membership in the church. To me, this exposure also communicated tolerance on the part of the church. It was refreshing to be shown how others practiced their faiths and to understand that there exist many paths to spiritual depth.

If your child asks questions about his place in the world or why he matters or what difference he can make, these are questions around spirituality. You can certainly draw on religious interpretations to further the discussion if appropriate. But it is not necessary. Be on the lookout for opportunities to engage around these questions. Spiritual inclination, like any other, if not nurtured, can wither.

For the child to emerge as a whole person, it is important to acknowledge this spiritual aspect of humanness. Parents who observe a child's interest, be it in math or sports or art, often encourage it. Spirituality should be no different.

ETHICS

According to the Pew Research Center's most recent study on the religious landscape in the United States, about 30 percent of adults seldomly or never attend religious services. Another 33 percent attend a few times a year. At the same time, 59 percent state feeling a deep sense of spiritual peace and well-being at least once a week. Another 46 percent report feeling a sense of wonder about the universe as often.[33]

For better or worse, religion has played a role in how we interact with one another by immersing adherents in certain prescribed sets of ethical guidelines. With more adults moving away from organized religion, their children are no longer inheriting these codes for interpersonal behavior in the same manner.[34] Even without a regular weekly religious practice, it is important to take a stand on what ethical, moral behavior will look like for you and your family.

If you are embarking on these spiritual and ethical questions outside of the direction of organized religious traditions, it is especially important to discuss alternatives and the outcomes of alternatives. These considerations are hardly ever decided in a vacuum, and you never know what other signals your child may be picking up from TV, games, movies, or other media.

Rather than trying to force a child to accept beliefs about a particular topic, for example, sharing or bullying, parents can have a conversation to explore behaviors and the outcomes associated with each: "You're choosing this and not that. Why is that? Why might one choice be preferable to another? How does it impact how you feel now and down the road? How about those around you?"

Of course, such a conversation should take into consideration the age and understanding of the child. A parent is probably not going to have a conversation like this with a three-year-old. Even so, parents can encourage young children to ask questions and actively think about their values and their role in the world rather than dictating these decisions for them. It is important for parents to encourage their children to have a more active role in choosing what they stand for as human beings. The key thread, again, is to nurture curiosity and compassion.

TOOL KIT FOR NURTURING SPIRITUALITY AND ETHICAL BEHAVIOR

At the beginning of this tool kit, we offer two important reminders for nurturing spirituality:

152 · RAISING GRITTY KIDS

1. Be open to your child's questions. View them as an opportunity for conversation and exploration with your child.
2. It is okay to say "I don't know" if you do not have a good answer in the moment. You can turn it around and engage your child by saying something like, "I don't know. What do you think? What have you observed? How are you feeling about this?"

REACH OUT

Parenting your child in a responsive way sometimes requires help from others. You may not have a strong spiritual leaning, but perhaps someone in your circle does. If you recognize your child has deep questions and would benefit from connecting with someone who thinks along the same lines, reach out to your circle.

READ BOOKS

If you are not sure where to start in thinking about ethical questions, let alone in communicating with your child about them, you might start with reading some spiritual writings on your own. If you are not drawn to any particular practice or school of thought, or if you are simply looking for a nonreligious type of ethical direction, there are many excellent Stoic writings about how to lead a life well lived. Marcus Aurelius's *Meditations* might be a place to start, and there are many accessible translations available today, including some with explanations and suggestions for added reflection.

In many ways, Joseph Campbell foresaw the generalized search for meaning that has become increasingly important as parts of society move away from organized religion. He recognized that many questions we ask ourselves are universal in nature and most will consider them at some point in their lives. The 1988 documentary *Joseph Campbell and the Power of Myth* comprises six hours of interviews on numerous spiritual topics, including the path of spiritual awakening, the relationship between humans and nature, spirituality and its power to help us make sense of the world, finding your purpose, and more.

While these suggestions are more aimed at the parent, with a child, *Aesop's Fables* and other books that address moral/ethical issues and how to think about them can be a great place to begin.

UNDERSTAND PROS AND CONS

In America people love happy endings, where everything works out, the hero wins, and human decency prevails. But life is not so simple. For the purposes of resiliency, it is important to help children understand that doing good has rewards, but there can be costs as well. When they are faced with an ethical choice and thinking about options, help them see the potential challenges and negative outcomes that go with making the morally right choice.

For a younger child, a big ethical issue could be seeing another child bullied, teased, or left out, or watching someone mistreat an animal. If the child steps in and says, "No, don't do that," she could lose a friend or be ostracized by the group.

Even a child of four or five might be faced with a situation like this in school or playing with kids in the neighborhood. When David was around six years old, he had an experience where another child wanted to take his pet rabbit and put it in the street so a car could run it over. David, expressing his extreme concern, later told our mom he did not want to spend time with that child anymore. Even then, he had a sensibility about right and wrong, his own values and ethics, and he made a decision based on his conviction.

ETHICAL ACTION

Volunteering broadens a child's perspective and helps her see the world beyond herself to become aware of the lives, situations, and needs of others. Helping around the house can be a way to introduce very young children to volunteering. This is a legitimate form of service learning.

The best way to teach children the importance of volunteering is to model it yourself. If you volunteer in a capacity where it would be appropriate to bring your child along, do so. I used to volunteer at our local conservatory. When I would go for service days, I would take Lena along to help clean up, weed, and organize scraps for composting, thus showing her the value of respect for the environment.

When taking children on field trips, my mom would say, "Ouch!" whenever one intentionally tugged at a bush, grabbed the limb of a tree, or plucked the petals from a flower. Trying to explain to a small child that plants, like humans, can be injured through our actions can be pretty tough. But most children understand the meaning of "ouch," and it can be a way to get them thinking of other living things.

Consider bringing your child along if you volunteer in an assisted living facility or visit the elderly. Doing so can help your child develop a respect for people in general, and for the elderly and lonely in particular.

Before you go, talk to your child about bringing something to let the person you are visiting know people are thinking of him. When we visit friends, family, or acquaintances, Lena and I look at drawings or artwork she has done recently and talk about which would be best to share. Now, Lena is starting to initiate this idea of sharing and giving on her own. She often tells my mom on the phone, "I'm drawing something beautiful for you and it's going to make you so happy." Or she sets aside cookies and other treasured snacks to share with my parents.

Another area where children can be brought into active participation around ethical questions is in donating extra toys or clothes. From time to time, Lena and I will go through objects that have been relegated to the back of the closet and decide which she would be willing to give away. We talk about the joy some other little child might get from a dress that no longer fits or books that Lena has outgrown. Through our conversation and by having her actively engaged, my hope is that Lena is learning generosity, compassion, and respect for others. By letting her guide the decision-making, I also get an opportunity to learn more about what she values and why.

REFLECTION

Make time for quiet reflection with your children. Lay out a blanket in the living room, lie down, and stare at the ceiling. Or take the blanket to a park, and stare at the sky or the trees. With the pervasiveness of digital technology, being still and doing nothing but observing is becoming a lost art.

If you have several children all engaged in different activities, it might be hard to find a space of five minutes for quiet reflection with each one. If they are on different sleep and wake schedules, you could work with this timing to plan a little quiet time alone with each child. In doing so, you teach a practice that some children will latch onto, which may spur their own spiritual growth.

A bit of uninterrupted quiet while driving in the car can provide valuable space for your child to share concerns or questions. Young children also can engage in drawing as a form of reflection, and as they get older, it might transition to writing and journaling.

SPIRITUALITY IS A GIFT

In my opinion, spirituality comes as a gift. It's probably something that you can't teach, and if a parent recognizes it in a child, carefully nourishing it would be the wise thing to do. Some people are a bit put off when unusual sensitivity is detected in a child. However, in some cases it may be an indication of a gift. My feeling is that Kara, along with several other family members, has that special gift.

When Kara was fourteen or fifteen, she volunteered as a reader for the blind. As an adult, Kara took a family acquaintance who was not fluent in English to an oral surgeon so she could help translate. I asked Kara why she was helping this woman when she had so many other work and family obligations, and she said, "She needs help and it would be a good thing to do." She had this deep sense of connection that moved her to help others however she could.

Several years ago, it was my honor, as a docent at the Field Museum, to

NURTURING SPIRITUALITY AND ETHICAL BEHAVIOR · 157

attend a special appearance of the Dalai Lama. Before attending, out of curiosity, I researched how the Dalai Lama is chosen. It was interesting to find that the search for the right boy can go on for years. My seat was very close to this wise, patient, and gentle man who at the same time, exuded strength and power. Being in his presence left me almost mesmerized.

Like with any talent or gift, the degree of intensity can vary from mild to mighty. In any case, as with exceptional musical ability, exceptional athletic ability, math, art, so it is with spirituality. In my opinion, when a wonderful gift is shared, the entire world stands to benefit.

● ●

JOURNEY WITH YOUR CHILD

In defining ourselves in spiritual, ethical, and moral terms, we start to understand ourselves as individuals. Having a solid foundation in this spiritual/ethical realm will influence the choices a child makes in other aspects of life, including choice of friends, career, and lifestyle.

As a parent, exploring spiritual questions with your child is an opportunity to explore them for yourself. If you have lost some of your own awe with the world around you, your child can help you to reconnect with the innocence and beauty of unfettered wonder and curiosity.

Next, we consider money and raising resilient kids, a topic nearly as complex and emotionally charged as spirituality.

158 · RAISING GRITTY KIDS

CHAPTER 8

Money and Raising Resilient Kids

"It is in no man's power to have whatever he wants; but he has it in his power not to wish for what he hasn't got, and cheerfully make the most of the things that do come his way."

—SENECA, LETTER CXXIII

When we were growing up, our mom used to joke with us that "the money coooooommmmmes, the money goes!" As I child, I internalized that message to mean that making money takes a lot of time and effort, and once you have it, it gets spent quickly because living comes with expenses. As an adult, I have worked hard to retool my view of money in part because I want to pass along a slightly different message to Lena. My general philosophy now is more along the lines of, "We can always make more money to afford XYZ. Let's figure out how we can!"

The bottom line is that as a parent, you have to know yourself, know what you value, and then evaluate your language, your messages, and your choices to ensure they are aligned with those stated values.

In our household, my husband and I tend to value experiences and quality time over things. However, I have friends who are more focused on material goods. One couple I know presented each of their children, son and daughter alike, with expensive gold necklaces on their first birthdays. When asked about it, they shared that they viewed it as an early investment for the children. The kids, like their parents, are always dressed to the nines and have all the latest gadgets and toys. It is certainly fun to visit because Lena gets to try out all these new marvels, but it can sometimes lead to tough conversations with her afterward. I find it most difficult to look into those pleading eyes and explain why I am not running out to buy the "it" thing of the moment.

Let's be real. It is not easy to stand firm when your choices look different from people around you. At Lena's school, parents had been one-upping each other, with the birthday party offerings getting more and more extravagant. It started out as simple cake and snacks for the guest of honor. Then, a parent convinced the director that a surprise visit from a clown during class would be fun. Not to be outdone, another parent brought in both Elsa and Anna to circulate among the children. (For those blissfully unaware, those are the main characters in Disney's *Frozen* franchise.) From Lena's reports, it sounded like the children were enjoying themselves immensely, but with birthdays seemingly every week, some parents were advocating for banning the parties altogether.

As Lena's birthday drew close, I hoped that we would still be able to have a class party for her. I wanted something special, but still educational, that would have all the children equally engaged. I opted for a party with a practitioner of rabbit therapy, which is a form of animal-assisted interaction that

160 · RAISING GRITTY KIDS

helps children develop gross and fine motor skills, eye-hand coordination, spatial orientation, concentration, teamwork, and emotional regulation through play with hugely fluffy and adorable bunnies.

Upon hearing my plans, a good friend asked unironically if maybe I could also have a clown come or, at a minimum, bring in some parrots from the local exotic bird house to liven things up. No, I assured her, no need for all that. I wanted the children to have a different birthday party experience, one, hopefully, they would remember for days, maybe even weeks to come. From all indications, the children did have a nice time learning about bunnies, feeding them by hand, and at the end, getting the chance to sit with a bunny on their laps. There was delicious cake and ice cream too, but, alas, no clowns.

My husband and I know what we value, and we are making choices that communicate those values to our daughter. For us, it really is primarily about experiences.

One of the main points in this chapter, as has been emphasized throughout the book, is that you must decide what is best for you and your child. Your preferences and decisions around money are uniquely yours. With the suggestions in this chapter, I hope to help take out some of the emotion that may be swirling around the very idea of money, so it can be viewed as a tool for facilitating experiences and learning rather than primarily as a marker of worth or status. The tool kit at the end provides suggestions for organically teaching children about money and how to use it.

KNOW YOUR VALUES

I absolutely love to travel and even as a child, I spent a fair amount of time fantasizing about and planning my next grand adventure. In our immediate family, we especially value time spent together exploring different cultures on these excursions. Back home, months or years down the road, it is great fun to look at the photographs and reminisce about the shared experience. Money is the tool that makes it possible.

As mentioned earlier, I know people who spend their money differently and in accordance with their priorities. As a parent, the most important part is knowing your values and then thinking about how you are communicating those to your child through your choices around money and elsewhere.

Understand that even if you actively choose not to think about what you value, your values are being transmitted to your kids through your choices. You are your child's first role model, and that is no small deal. Better to think consciously through the kind of messages you want to send. Fair warning: it can require a deep level of introspection around your own beliefs about money and what role it plays in your life, but it is worth the effort.

If you are parenting with a partner, it is a good idea to share your individual views on money, as uncomfortable as having this conversation might be. If there are fundamental or seemingly insurmountable differences, say if one partner believes money is the root of all evil and the other is focused on saving and investing, you might need outside help to address that issue.

However, if your differences are minor—say, one of you

values spending money on house remodeling and the other enjoys spending it on vacations—it is important to come to a compromise through understanding and respecting the other person's preferences. As has been highlighted, people have different values, and that is okay. After partners have discussed how they view money and how they want to spend it, they can talk about the values they would like their child to have and start to engage the child in these discussions as well. This is a fantastic opportunity to learn more about your child and what he has already learned from watching you.

One final and very important note: if partners have disagreements about how money is being spent, those are best conducted behind closed doors, not in front of the child. One key responsibility of parents is to provide protection and a safe place for the child. It can be disconcerting for a child to overhear a discussion that may bring into question the fundamental stability of her environment.

ECONOMIC EDUCATION

Following the 2008 economic crash, Kara and I had a conversation about my financial status. "So, how prepared are you?" she asked. "Do you have your game plan? Are you willing to take the actions needed to protect your capital? Do you know the steps you need to take to get prepared? It's not hard to do, but it does take some commitment on your part." These questions are even more meaningful in this time of COVID-19.

For decades, economic education has been neglected and many welcome a chance to learn more. In doing so, you will not only gain useful information but will also become confident when helping your children.

On its website (econedlink.org), the Council for Economic Education states its challenge: "In America, we spend billions of dollars helping our children master reading, writing, and arithmetic. And we send them out into the world lacking the basic skills to prosper in life: understanding personal finance and economics." The site goes on to highlight that one out of six students in the United States does not reach the baseline of proficiency in financial literacy. One out of four millennials spend more than they earn. Sixty-seven percent of Generation Y have less than three months of emergency funds. Given the recent COVID-19 crisis, these stats take on new meaning.

The council's website provides a number of excellent activities for parents and children. There is a Financial Fitness for Life parent's guide in which incentives and activities are provided for kindergarten through grade 5 and for grades 6 through 12, in both English and Spanish. The K–5 section, for example, starts with the question, "Do these words sound familiar to you? 'I want that. Why can't I have that? All of my friends have one.'" The site then goes on to talk about how to address statements like this with your child.

The guide also includes information on other potentially touchy topics: do young children need to know...where money comes from? How workers earn money? What entrepreneurship is? How to count money? Of course, the answer to all of the aforementioned is yes, and this guide provides information to get you started.

In addition to information on earning income, the section for grades 6 through 12 discusses money management, saving, spending, and using credit, as well as terms such as opportunity cost, incentive, disincentive, and consequence. The guide also includes simple, practical ideas for implementing strategies around these topics.

For me, learning about how our economy works was a welcomed expe-

164 · RAISING GRITTY KIDS

rience. A lot of my education came through programs designed to fill education gaps in economics. Some was inspired by my daughter's early interest in financial matters.

. . . .

USE MONEY AS A TOOL

We all live in a world where money has a function. It is a tool that enables activities, both obligatory and discretionary. For children to be resilient and able to interact in this world, they must have money skills.

VALUES AND MONEY

As mentioned earlier, my sister had a discerning eye for quality workmanship. This trait expressed itself as an appreciation for name brand clothing, shoes, and purses. When Nora was a teen, our mom encouraged her to distinguish between a genuine love of craftmanship and a desire for the latest labels borne more out of pressure from peers to conform. It is very likely that some of both was at play.

Our mom explained that she would pay a certain amount and Nora would have to pay the difference. Nora knew what was important to her and because our mom had laid out the guidelines, she also learned the cost in both time and money for things of exceptional value. She understood the trade-off and she opted to exchange her time on weekends, working at a nearby boutique, in order to purchase the items she wanted. Later, our mom began to understand that it was indeed more about craftmanship than anything else. As an adult and a frugal young mother, my sister learned to sew

MONEY AND RAISING RESILIENT KIDS · 165

and knit both to save money and to make items that met her standards.

When I was in elementary school, I decided I wanted to get really serious with my violin studies. I had auditioned with the top teachers in Chicago and one had accepted me on the condition that I get a new violin—he had commented to my mom that what I was playing was in truth, a VSO, a violin-shaped object, and it had to go. Buying a violin worthy of the work required to advance to the next level of proficiency required money.

My parents understood how important playing violin was to me. They saw the hours I put in: three or four a day, in addition to my demanding school studies and not including extra hours in orchestra rehearsals. They witnessed the drive that compelled me to keep at it in spite of the stress of performances and competitions. They understood my deep desire to perfect my technique so that I could play the challenging pieces that before had eluded me. To that end, they were willing to invest in a new violin.

In the end, finding the perfect violin was an experience in itself. After visiting many instrument dealers and testing a range of violins, new and old, we decided to have one made by one of the foremost violinmakers in the United States. He actually made three violins just for me and gave me the opportunity to choose the one I wanted. My mom and I got a chance to follow the process step-by-step, from the selection of wood for the violin bodies, to the gouging and finishing, all the way to the varnishing.

Over the course of about eighteen months, we regularly visited his shop to see the progress on the instruments. I still have and play that violin, and I still have a relationship with the maker. That violin allowed me to play in orchestras and tour different countries when I was in school, to play chamber music for enjoyment years after I quit studying, and to make new friends and acquaintances in the process. The experiences gained went far beyond the cost of the violin and the lessons themselves.

ORGANIC PARENTING ACTIVITIES

Part of our mom's organic parenting style involves the idea that anything in the child's world is fair game for promoting curiosity and learning. Related to money, Mom seized on situations where we could learn about things like taxes, the value of time versus money, and other fundamental principles needed to ensure we would one day manage our own finances successfully. In the process, we got real-life opportunities to hone practical math skills like basic arithmetic, rounding and estimation, checking totals, and more.

For example, when our mom took us to the grocery store, she taught us about money in a couple of different ways, which came up organically as part of the shopping experience. We might play a game of Do You Have Enough Money? Our mom would give each of us a few dollars to spend. When we picked out an item, she would ask, "Do you have enough money to buy that?" Then we would have to find the price tag and do the math. If we came back with a few items, we would have to figure out if we could afford them all and if not, which ones to put back to stay within budget. This was great fun for us and was our mom's clever way to encourage analytical skills and decision-making, while giving us autonomy to make the final choice. It was satisfying to reach the register and discover we had indeed figured out the correct total. At the same time, our mom caught a glimpse into what we valued, what we were adamant about keeping, and what we were willing to put back. It also kept us well occupied while our mom completed the bulk of the shopping.

Another game we played as we got older was Total the Cart. As we put things on the conveyor belt, we would guesstimate the prices, round them up, and keep a running tally in our heads. At the end, we would compete to see who was closest to the final amount. In addition to practicing our mental math, we gained a sense of the relative cost of food items.

As a result of these organic activities and the discussions that followed, my siblings and I understood what things cost—from a new pair of shoes all the way to a college education. By the time we reached high school, we each sought out scholarships and grants to earn money for tuition. Our parents had not asked, but we wrote essays, filled out applications, signed up for competitions—basically did whatever we could to earn money to help pay for our education.

EXPERIENCES

Studies have shown that people derive a greater sense of well-being from spending money on experiences, rather than things. The good feelings that accompany objects tends to be short-lived, whereas one can revisit photos, memories, and even lessons from experiences, which become part of who one is in ways that objects cannot.

That said, even money spent on material things can be turned into an experience. For example, if a family value is to be dressed a certain way, parents can turn clothes shopping into a shared event. Talk about what it would take to put together a certain outfit. Follow this with an excursion to the store. Try on the clothes and pay attention to the details that set one outfit apart from another. Focus on the quality and workmanship. Help the child articulate why she prefers one dress over another—is it the color, the texture, the pattern? There are many ways to deepen the experience around shopping if you have a bit of fun with it.

In the positive psychology movement, several studies have been done to answer the question, "How much money do you need to be happy?" What researchers have found is that the sweet spot is having enough to cover basic expenses—in Maslow's Hierarchy of Needs, the bottom levels of food, shelter, and safety net—plus some extra. In other words, it does improve well-being to avoid stress and anxiety by having enough money to cover emergencies and unexpected expenses, but accumulating for accumulation's sake does not seem to add to people's happiness.

"It has been said that man's greatest delight is to possess things. No. Man's greatest delight is using them, using them to perfect himself and at the same time to improve his environment."
—MARIA MONTESSORI, *EDUCATION AND PEACE*

TAKE EMOTION OUT OF THE EQUATION

I have friends who are brilliant and accomplished, and simultaneously terrified of money issues. They are plagued by questions like, "How do I know if I budgeted properly? How do I know which credit card payment I should make first? Will I have enough money at the end of the month?" Their stress is palpable.

By being exposed to money concepts early and often, my siblings and I do not have this level of anxiety about money. This is not to say I have not had my fair share of lean years when I worked long and hard hours and only had the time and money to order off the dollar menu. However, I always felt like I was armed with the tools that would help me make choices in order to improve things, even if slowly and only incrementally.

My parents were always open about income, paying taxes, and general information on what it meant to be an adult from a financial perspective, and it had a grounding effect. Even in the face of terrible financial decisions, of which I have made plenty, I have been able to move through the fear and feelings of overwhelm, to keep taking action in order to resolve the situation. This is a direct result of the resilience and self-confidence I have gained from other areas of life.

One of the worst traps people sometimes fall into is associating money with self-worth. It can turn into a cycle of feeling on top of the world when you have money in your pocket and then terrible when the balances read zero. If you can step back and see money as a tool, one of many at your disposal, this can help to put money back into perspective. It takes the emotion out of it, which can allow a healthier relationship toward it.

MONEY TOOL KIT

The more parents know and understand their child—her view of money, her values, and her inclinations—the better they can prepare that child for the future in a way that works for her. Knowing the child is what lays the groundwork for building resiliency.

The following tools can help you work with your child to provide a healthy view of money.

BUILD AN EXPERIENCE

No matter what the budget, parents should think in terms of providing rich experiences for their children. Not only can a shared adventure provide mental stimulation for the child, it can also be a springboard for connection around more emotional or social topics.

If money is of concern, there are often low-cost and even free family-fun activities in most locales. Some cities provide summer concerts in the park, free family movie nights, or other activities. Depending on where you live, you might have access to museums, planetariums, arboretums, parks, open spaces, nature trails, play productions, athletic events, library events, and more. It might require a bit of preplanning as free or discounted hours may be very specific, but it can be well worth the effort. All of these activities can help to broaden the child's understanding of the world and his place in it.

Exposing kids to varied experiences may also provide points of conversation and connection when they are interacting out in the world. I have a vivid memory of going to the Spertus Museum of Judaica as a child, where they put on mock archeological digs for kids. Later in life, I mentioned to a new friend the joy I had in visiting the museum and she was duly impressed that I had been when many in our cosmopolitan city were unaware of its existence and importance. In some ways, I believe our friendship was cemented through this acknowledgment of mutual interest in each other's cultural heritage. The more experiences a child has to draw on, the more potential connections she will have with others, including those who may be quite different. Having a broad and diverse network later in life is important because you never know from whom a critical connection may originate.

Here is a list of fun activities that may be right in your backyard:

- Science museums, planetariums, aquariums, zoos, nature conservatories, art museums, etc. As a result of the COVID-19 lockdowns, many museums have developed new and expanded online programs. Chicago's Field Museum of Natural History, for example, has teacher-developed programs for children and parents. Another option to explore is Google's collection of images and tours from over two thousand museums around the world. Check it out here: https://artsandculture.google.com/.
- Libraries. Many public libraries have free resources, such as museum passes. Other libraries, like the Newberry, have wonderful online resources for parents. Additionally, there may be regularly hosted story hours or other book-related events like scavenger hunts and children's theater.
- Art organizations. Many arts organizations now have outreach to children and families. The Chicago Symphony, for example, has wonderful children's concerts, which aim to make classical music accessible to all. There are also youth-focused theater groups performing plays that can make for much engaging discussion with your little one.
- Local farms and orchards. Where Lena and I live, there are many small farmers who we visit to buy seasonal pro-

duce. We have even gone to visit the lady farmer who has a small stable of cows and provides fresh milk for making cheese. It is entirely possible that seeing these farm animals up close has contributed to Lena's interest in becoming vegetarian.

Some of you may look at this list and feel overwhelmed. Even though many are free or low-cost, it still takes time and energy, and that is by no means trivial. But incorporate what you can. Even if you visit a museum once or twice a year, those trips will have a terrific impact on your child.

EXPLORE AT-HOME PLAY OPTIONS

In keeping with the experience idea, you can create your own play options from what you have at home, making an event out of the whole activity: coming up with the plan, finding the supplies, and getting to work. The number of low-cost play options is truly endless, limited only by your creativity. Here are a few ideas to get you started.

Recycled Items

Use recycled items—cans, straws, Popsicle sticks—to make things. As mentioned earlier, empty canned good cans can be used to create homemade instruments. To create different sounds, kids might fill the cans with different items: dried beans, rice, marbles, whatever you have on hand. A bigger can could be used as a drum with wooden spoons as the sticks. Use your new instruments to put on a performance for family.

Making and Growing

I have found that making things, even simple things, has given me a hearty appreciation for how much goes into the act of building something. Simple projects like turning old socks into puppets for a puppet show require minimal objects but can provide hours of learning and fun. If you have never tried gardening with your child, that can also be very rewarding. You do not have to commit to a major outdoor project. Even the experience of planting a few bean pods in a moistened paper towel within a paper cup can be awe-inspiring to the young mind.

Monthly Box Service

I subscribe to a monthly box service that sends kits for children to make their own toys. One kit had the makings for a little purse that required some simple sewing and decorating. Part of the fun for Lena was in carrying the purse around and telling those who admired it that she had made it herself.

Fair warning: your child's peers (and sometimes parents) may make fun of the low-tech nature of these handmade projects. This has happened to us on more than one occasion. In those situations, I used it as an opportunity to talk to Lena about our family values and what she thinks is important.

VOLUNTEERING AND SHARING

Volunteering and sharing both have a role in developing resiliency by increasing a child's engagement, self-confidence, and compassion for others. Whether one is donating time or money, the focus is looking beyond one's own personal needs.

Sharing financially involves making choices about where to

allocate money and in what fashion. The same goes for volunteering time. This is a powerful choice for children to be exposed to, and an area where parents can give kids some autonomy in decision-making. Children generally do not have a say in where the family lives or what furniture or groceries the family buys, but they can have a say in something like giving to charity.

When David was about eight, he decided to donate the entire contents of his piggy bank, about forty dollars, to a charity through an event at school. Our mom only found out when his teacher called to double-check that it was okay. He did not ask our mom, not because he was trying to hide what he was doing, but rather because he simply knew it was something he wanted to do. After talking it over with him, our mom okayed the donation.

RESOURCES

As my mom has mentioned, the Council for Economics Education's website (https://www.councilforeconed.org/) is a great place to start for ideas related to money and economics. The website has recommended books and references on economics in children's literature, US history, and more.

HAVE A PLAN

To help your child develop a healthy relationship with money—to view it as a tool, understand how it works, relate to it without emotion—you need a plan. Your plan may not look the same as your neighbor's, and that is to be expected. As long as you are on the same page as your partner, or at least understand and respect one another's values, you are on the right track.

Look for everyday situations to talk to your children about money—at the grocery store, at the bank, as you pay bills. By talking to children early and often, you remove potential anxiety around money, building emotional resiliency in the process.

In this chapter, we talked about the importance of building connections with your child through experiences. In the next chapter, we explore the importance of maintaining experiences and interests apart from your child, so you don't lose yourself in your parenting.

CHAPTER 9

Don't Lose Yourself in Your Parenting

"Self-care is the internal hard work of making tough decisions for yourself and by yourself...But, in my experience, facing those growing pains directly pays off multiple times over."

—POOJA LAKHSHMIN

Lena is a winter baby, and when spring finally arrived in Chicago, I regularly strapped her into the baby carrier and walked around our neighborhood and down to the local park to get fresh air and take in the sights.

One spring day, I put Lena in her stroller and we walked to the park, where I came upon a group of young moms with their kids. It seemed like many of them knew each other. As Lena dozed, I sat not far from the group, catching snippets of the conversation. From what I gathered, the discussion revolved around all things kiddie—this diaper, that feeding schedule, how they were managing a certain dietary restriction, how one pediatrician's waiting room compared to another's in terms of cleanliness and toy offerings. They covered the gamut of baby-related topics, and seemingly, little else.

At that point in my life, I had newly launched a business and had many of those concerns on my mind, in addition to raising my child. I wondered what it would be like to spend my days completely focused on Lena and baby things. Could I even do that? If I'm truthful, the answer is probably not. Even at the park, I found myself slipping into thoughts of other things as I gently rocked Lena's stroller.

Parents have to figure out what works for them—going back to work, staying at home, working part time, working from home, sending young children to day care, or not. No matter which path you choose, it is important to keep some part of yourself separate from your children. Put another way, try not lose yourself in your parenting.

Parenting provides an unrivaled opportunity for learning, self-reflection, and growth. We encourage you to embrace the experience of parenthood, the new perspectives you gain and the lessons you learn, and bring that learning to the other aspects of your life. Especially in the early days, it can be difficult to maintain a life apart from your children, but ultimately, doing so is beneficial for parents and children alike. This chapter discusses why this is the case and provides ideas for making it happen.

IMPORTANCE OF SELF-CARE

There are several reasons parents should take care not to lose themselves in their parenting. Here we highlight a few of the most important.

WELL-BEING OF THE CHILD

It is a slippery slope to overactive parenting when the child becomes a parent's sole purpose. This can lead to a parent unintentionally hindering the child's ability to express herself and exert autonomy. Years later, this can result in a young adult who lacks the tools to cope with an uncertain future and feels unready to launch.

By developing relationships and interests outside the home and apart from the child, parents interrupt the tendency toward helicopter parenting. They also reduce the risk of long-term separation anxiety in the child. By practicing separation gradually and consistently—by literally separating from the child to attend book club or go to the gym—the parent gives the young child space to learn that he is separate from the parent and that is okay.

CHILD'S FIRST ROLE MODEL

Consciously or not, a child looks to her parents as a model of what it means to be an adult. To the extent that parents want to raise children who are well-rounded, contributing members of society, it is important to consider what one is modeling for them.

As role models, parents demonstrate both the benefits and the responsibilities of adulthood. It is true that once one becomes a parent, childrearing and the well-being of the child become a significant point of focus. However, your child should also see you doing the things that identify you as a real, live person with interests, hopes, and dreams that are entirely your own.

FIRST ROLE MODEL

As parents, first and foremost, we want our children to be whole human beings. Of course, we want a lot of other things for them as well, such as confidence to pursue their ambitions. As the child's first role model, the parent should not neglect his or her own growth in terms of mental and physical well-being.

As much as we try to assume the responsibility placed on us by our enlightened founders, the truth is we can't always predict or guarantee outcomes, especially when so many variables are involved. What you can do is constantly work on those things that make you feel complete and bring joy to your life. The child benefits from watching you laugh and have fun, as well as seeing how you cope with failures or challenges.

When my sister was a toddler, our mom was considering a change in career path and needed to complete a physics class to move forward. She considered how best to manage attending class when childcare was not available. She knew Nora was capable of playing quietly with Legos or other toys, so she asked the instructor if she could bring my sister to class. Gaining new knowledge and expertise was important for our mom on a professional level, and she found a way to make it compatible with her parenting. She was modeling adult behavior to my sister by pursuing her own goals, navigating obstacles, taking responsibility, and finding solutions. At four, my sister gained her first experience in a university classroom, and she still remembers sitting quietly in the back of the room as our mom participated in class.

WELL-BEING OF PARENTS

There is a reason most people are drawn to hobbies and activities. Becoming a parent does not suddenly flip a switch and turn off these interests. These intellectual, artistic, or physical pursuits should be nurtured after children come along. Participation might look different than before, but it can and should still happen.

For years, I have been privileged to have a friendship with a brilliant woman who loves to discuss topics such as spirituality, self-actualization, and identity. Like me, she is a voracious reader, consuming business and philosophy books alike, and we regularly exchange ideas around what we have read. Now that my friend is a new mom, there is an added depth to our discussions, particularly as she has witnessed in real time her own priorities shifting.

Discussions with trusted friends, new and old, on a range of topics can help one make sense of the world, and such connections should not be neglected. Just remember that if you invest all of your time and energy into your child, it can be especially difficult to adjust once that child has left home.

. . . .

THE EMPTY NEST

My generation heard a lot of chatter about the empty nest. Exactly what is the etymology of the term? Apparently, the term *empty-nest syndrome* appeared in 1965 when a team of researchers presented their findings on the "psychosocial aspects of conflict between depressed women and their grown children" at the 121st annual meeting of the American Psychiatric Association. The condition is described with words like *depression, feeling of isolation, sadness,* and *excessive worry.* "Depression and the end of child rearing became inexorably linked in the media following this study, spawning a plethora of subsequent studies and books which perpetuated the notion that women, like female birds, had served their primary purpose when their offspring left the home (nest) and went off to make their way in the world alone without their parents."[35]

Thankfully, we no longer put women out to pasture after their child-rearing days are done. Today, there are numerous articles advising couples about what to do when they are empty-nesters. One article in the *Huffington Post* gave several tips to help parents experiencing this ailment:

- Remind yourself it's very normal to feel sad and to miss your child.
- Redefine your child's leaving. See the opportunity to do things that you were unable to do before.
- Stay connected to the child through email.
- Don't hesitate to lean on friends and colleagues for support.
- Initiate self-care and do nice things for yourself on a routine basis. Get a massage. Take a yoga or art class. Take a mini-vacation. Tend to your garden. Go to the gym.
- Don't try to accelerate recovery. Allow grieving to run its course. Don't make major changes like selling the house or moving to another state. You might want to go to a family guidance counselor.
- Do volunteer work. Feel purposeful again.[36]

Most of you reading this book are likely still in the child-raising stage. How can you avoid the empty-nest syndrome? Part of the answer can be found by starting at the end of those seven tips above and working backward.

Here are some examples:

One should not wait for kids to leave home to do volunteer work routinely.

182 · RAISING GRITTY KIDS

Learning how to grieve should be a part of ongoing life learning. A young person's leaving home should be more about anticipation and curiosity around the next stage of his life. What is more, though it may be a hands-off moment, it should not mean the end of checking in to see how things are going.

Getting a massage, yoga, and art classes should be a part of adult life even during parenting. Perhaps not as often or as intensely as when there's more time, but these things can be done reasonably.

Self-care is indirectly instructive for the child. It's healthy on a number of levels. Consider things like attending a concert or going to a game with your friends; visiting certain museums or having a girls night out for dinner; learning a new language or a new field of study; taking up cooking, running, or painting.

Regarding leaning on friends and colleagues, it can be said that this, too, is something that should be ongoing throughout adulthood. Cultivating friendships, some of which may change over time, is a life skill. Learning compatibility with colleagues is too.

. . . .

OPPORTUNITY TO REMEMBER YOUR OWN HISTORY

Especially as children get older, parents have an opportunity to share authentically who they are, what excites them, and the formative experiences that have shaped their worldview. My mom spent a lot of time sharing history about herself and others in the family. Her stories gave me a sense of grounding, of having come from a long line of thinkers and doers. Most importantly, they provided a launching point for crafting my own identity in the world and charting a path for my future.

DON'T LOSE YOURSELF IN YOUR PARENTING · 183

Perhaps your parents did not talk about themselves, their interests, their values, their life before kids, and you may be wondering how to initiate these kinds of conversations with your own children. These sharing experiences can happen anytime. For example, if you and your son have a habit of going on walks together, you might talk about activities you participated in with your dad. While baking cupcakes with your daughter, you might share a memory of baking with your grandparents. One day, I was trying to re-create my grandmother's tuna salad recipe, the one she used to make whenever I was sick and stayed home from school. As I put the ingredients together, I told Lena how comforted I was, how cared for I felt, when my grandmother prepared these sandwiches.

My mom has embraced technology to help her stay in touch with all the grandkids. In a weekly family conference call with my sister and her children, they read books together and discuss movies or current events. My mom often makes connections between what they discuss and my sister's childhood, telling the grands, "Well, you might not believe it, but when your mother was that age, she…" These brief discussions give children a sense of who their parents are and where they came from. As you and your child read books, enjoy plays, attend sporting events, and watch TV shows or movies, you might think of connections to your own childhood. What were your favorite books? Or bands? What memorable events happened in your community when you were growing up? What do you remember shaping your thinking at the time?

GIVE CHILDREN PERSPECTIVE

Many young children cannot imagine their parents as having

184 · RAISING GRITTY KIDS

been young. Letting kids in on this secret can be quite helpful, especially when something not-so-great happens. I sometimes tell my daughter, "Oh, that happened to me too. It's okay. It's not a forever thing." By sharing your own experiences as a child, you give your kids perspective on their current situation by letting them know that they are not alone in what they are experiencing.

This comes back to the idea of being a role model. Young children in particular may find comfort in knowing that Mom and Dad went through something similar and survived to tell the tale. No more bedwetting. No more being scared of the dark.

Parents know that certain freedoms are not appropriate at certain ages, but children on the receiving end may simply hear, "No, you can't do that." They might appreciate hearing that Mom and Dad understand their frustration, and that this, too, shall pass.

TOOL KIT FOR MAINTAINING YOUR PERSONHOOD

We have already covered several reasons why it is important to take time to care for yourself, but here are some suggestions on how to do it.

MAINTAIN FRIENDSHIPS WITH PEOPLE WHO DO NOT HAVE KIDS

Parents need friends who knew them before they had baby brain. These friends remind you of the crazy things you used to do when you were fun (not that I'm speaking from personal experience…).

In addition, these friends can be sources of conversation on nonchild-related topics. They can help you stay informed on what is hot and of the moment. They can tell you about the newest restaurants and the most bingeable shows. Even if you do not always have time to go out and do these things, there can be vicarious pleasure in hearing about the shenanigans of others.

START A FAMILY CIRCLE

With your friends who do have kids, try organizing a regular group that involves parents and children. When you have a bunch of adults in the room, it is much easier to watch the kids and have adult conversation because everyone is keeping an eye on what is going on.

My husband and I belonged to a supper club for seven years before any of the couples had children. Every month, a different couple would host everyone for an elaborate spread, and discussion that would go long into the night. As people started having babies, supper club morphed into a brunch club so that parents could bring their babies and still sit around the table and talk. It was a great chance to catch up and have a couple of hours of blissfully grown-up conversation.

MAINTAIN HOBBIES AND INTERESTS

Did you practice yoga before you had children? Take pottery classes? Play softball? Get back to it, whatever it is. If there is a new hobby you have wanted to try, see if you can incorporate that. You may not participate as frequently, but it is important to include some of the activities that bring you joy. Hobbies provide a much-needed opportunity for social interaction that is not focused on children.

TAKE YOUR CHILD TO WORK

To broaden your child's view of you, and if acceptable at your workplace, bring your child along for a short visit so she can see another environment where you spend time and interact with a whole different universe of people.

If your work is remote, and it would not be too disruptive, you could invite your child to join you for the first couple of minutes on a video call, when the greetings and small talk happen. Just be sure to have a plan for how to refocus on your meeting after those initial minutes have gone by! When Lena joins me, I usually have some workbooks and activities set up that she can do quietly on her own while I complete my call. I also set an expectation with her about the duration of the call and that I need quiet once the meeting begins in earnest. Usually, I also build in a little time after the call to take a break, to thank Lena for helping Mama get her work done, and to acknowledge the work she has completed on her own while I was talking.

I have a good friend who is a successful entrepreneur. He routinely brings his primary school-aged daughters along to business lunches, sometimes at fancy restaurants. He shared with me that he viewed it as early training, getting them comfortable with the ways in which business gets done. By letting them see him at work, he is modeling adulting for them, demonstrating what it means to make money and to pay bills.

TAKE CARE OF YOURSELF

Let's face it. As wonderful as it is to be a parent, it can also be overwhelming and exhausting. Devoting time to your own well-being is an overall benefit because if you are worn out and burnt out, you will not be as patient, observant, and responsive to your child's needs as you otherwise might be. Schedule some alone time to reinvigorate yourself, whether that means hiking solo for a couple hours, getting a massage, or going for a manicure. Also understand that sometimes self-care is less about doing a particular activity and more about exhibiting a certain behavior, like setting good boundaries. If you have energy leaks from certain enervating activities or people, self-care could very well look like saying no to those things more directly and more often.

REFLECT AND JOURNAL

Take opportunities to reflect on how parenting has changed you and journal your thoughts. Down the road, you can return to your entries and review what you were thinking and feeling at different points in time. You may be amazed at how your perspective shifts over time and how you have grown as a person.

Active reflecting can also provide a chance for you to better understand your parents' choices and their parenting journey.

There are so many things I was blind to before I had Lena: the overwhelming feeling of love for this tiny person, the energy-sapping vigilance required as she tested boundaries, the balancing act of being protective but letting her grow into new responsibilities. Becoming a mother unexpectedly opened the door to a new level of compassion for my parents as I gradually understood what it must have been like raising me.

Until I had a child, I was aware only vaguely of the impact my various hair-raising adventures might have had on my parents—hiking in faraway places with no ready access to medical treatment if something had gone terribly wrong, jumping out of airplanes, taking motorcycle lessons when I could not properly ride a bicycle. Looking back, my parents likely felt more than a little anxiety over many of my choices. When it became clear that Lena might be a daredevil in her own right, my mom smiled and said, "Ah, now you will understand."

SHARE INTERESTS WITH KIDS

What are you passionate about? Whether it is music, art, video games, cooking, books, movies, or soccer, sharing your passion with your child makes you a three-dimensional person. Even if your child cringes at the idea that Dad used to play in a band or Mom used to ice skate, it is still important for children to know their parents are people.

DATE NIGHT

Going out with your partner is an important part of maintaining your personhood apart from your child. In some ways, children are like little satellites. You need to get out of the house without your moons to remember what it is like to navigate the world unfettered. And chances are, you and your partner might need time to reconnect as adults too.

RESOURCES

I have three reading recommendations, two for you and your partner and one to read with a younger child:

- *The No-Cry Separation Anxiety Solution* by Elizabeth

Pantley has excellent information about what normal separation anxiety looks like in young children, the value of separation, and how to successfully separate.

- The article "Separation Anxiety and Separation Anxiety Disorder" (available at https://www.helpguide.org/articles/anxiety/separation-anxiety-and-separation-anxiety-disorder.htm) provides information to ease your mind about setting boundaries with your children, along with many excellent tips.
- *Llama Llama Misses Mama* by Anna Dewdney is a cute story about separation that you can read with your child to help him understand that being apart from Mom and Dad sometimes is a natural part of growing up.

GOOD FOR EVERYONE

Children who have a good sense of who they are tend to be more resilient in the face of change. Use the safe space of your home to help them develop this sense of self. Practicing separation consistently and in a controlled way is important for encouraging autonomy. Losing yourself in your parenting, helicopter parenting, and not letting children make decisions all inhibit the development of resilience.

Here's another mantra to remember: help your child by helping yourself. You should not feel guilty about going to the gym or meeting a friend for coffee from time to time. In making space for yourself, you are modeling what it looks like to be self-confident, to have self-respect, and to maintain your personhood.

Next, we consider the implications of parenting with others—your partner and beyond.

CHAPTER 10

Parenting with Others

"It's right to talk about motherhood as a wonderful thing, but we also need to talk about its stresses and strains. It's OK not to find it easy. Asking for help should not be seen as a sign of weakness."

—KATE MIDDLETON, DUCHESS OF CAMBRIDGE

My friend Robin is a busy working mother with two children under four. One of her values as a parent is to limit the amount of sugar her children consume, and family members who might watch her kids understand this preference.

One Saturday afternoon, Robin dropped her kids off at her parents' house so she could run some errands. She returned to the house a little earlier than expected. When Robin opened the door, her toddler ran toward her, chocolate smeared all over his face.

When Robin looked up, speechless, her parents turned toward her and said with a hint of glee, "Oh, you caught us!"

Grandparents want to be cool, they want to be loved, so they sometimes (intentionally or unintentionally) end up playing good cop to your bad cop. How fun is that for you? Parenting in a vacuum would be a challenging endeavor on its own, but no one parents in a vacuum. Grandparents, aunts, uncles, brothers, sisters, in-laws, friends, teachers, and coaches all interact with and to varying degrees influence your child. These individuals all bring differing histories, personalities, and philosophies to the table.

As a savvy parent, you need tools to help navigate potential pitfalls when parenting with others. This chapter offers ideas for developing your own parenting philosophy, determining your nonnegotiables, and deciding what to do when breakdowns inevitably happen. The chapter ends with key items to place in your parenting with others tool kit to help you reach the best outcomes for you and your child.

DEVELOPING YOUR PARENTING PHILOSOPHY

In chapter 2, we introduced the authoritarian and authoritative parenting styles in relation to knowing your child. Here, we will consider these parenting philosophies and two others in more detail so you and your partner can discuss and decide what works best for you and your children.

We want to emphasize that we are not advocating for some hypothetical perfect way to parent. However, we will point out that as it pertains to raising gritty kids, many well-documented studies have shown that authoritative parenting has the best long-term results.

PARENTING STYLES

In the 1960s, Diana Baumrind developed a framework around different parenting philosophies. She created a categorization of three parenting types plus one:

- Authoritarian/disciplinarian
- Permissive/indulgent
- Authoritative
- Uninvolved

In shorthand, Baumrind would say the authoritarian style is too harsh, the permissive style is too soft, and the authoritative style is just right. The "plus one" is uninvolved parenting, which is really nonparenting, but it is a legitimate style and does come with its own benefits and challenges.

Authoritarian/disciplinarian parenting involves a lot of rules, perhaps not always well explained, and not always consistent with the parent's own behavior. Think, "Do as I say, not as I do." Communication between parent and child tends to be unidirectional, from parent to child, rather than a dialogue. Authoritarian parents also tend to be low on nurturing (responsiveness) and high in expectations (demandingness).

Permissive/indulgent parenting is on the opposite end of the spectrum. Parents provide few rules and communication is open, but may lack direction. Permissive parents tend to be high in nurturing and low in expectations. They act more like friends than parents. Some people consider attachment parenting, where parents reorient their lives around a newborn and his needs, a special class of permissive parenting. Most psychologists agree that this is not exactly the case but

PARENTING WITH OTHERS · 193

it can lead to indulgent parenting if positive boundaries and discipline are not established.

Another philosophy that might fall into the permissive category is slow parenting. The idea here is that the child actively sets the pace in her world, exploring and discovering new things unimpeded by adults. The style is more permissive, but in its most positive forms, provides guardrails to ensure the child's safety.

Authoritative parenting is a balance between the first two styles. Parents provide clearly explained rules and engage in frequent age-appropriate dialogue with their child, receiving feedback both verbally and through observation of the child's behavior. Authoritative parenting is marked by high expectations and high nurturing.

Helicopter parenting is another form of child rearing that has gotten a lot of press in recent years. In this book, we use the term *helicopter parenting* to describe an overly involved, interventionist style. It typically involves high expectations in one particular area: performance, academic and otherwise.

Uninvolved parenting, as the name suggests, is when parents provide few rules, little communication, low nurturing, and low expectations. Free-range parenting, which is purposefully hands-off based on the idea that children will become independent by figuring things out on their own, is a more positive form of the uninvolved style. However, many do note that uninvolved parenting can devolve into neglect if it is too hands-off.

MOVING TOWARD "JUST RIGHT"

As mentioned earlier, studies have shown that the authoritative parenting style is the most effective in raising resilient children. It works because the parent is simultaneously setting out high expectations, engaging in dialogue, allowing autonomy while being present to make adjustments as necessary, and giving the child chances to build a life-skills tool kit in a safe environment. As Baumrind has said, authoritative parenting represents the Goldilocks scenario: the just right place where you want to land.

Achieving this perfect balance of challenging but attainable expectation with ongoing nurturing is harder for some people than others. Maybe you recognize that communication is not your strong suit. That is okay. You can work to engage your child in conversation. Maybe your parents had few rules, and you tend to swing between too few and too many. Maybe you are uncomfortable with discipline. Whatever the case may be, if you are aware of your natural parenting tendencies, you will be better able to course correct if necessary.

It is important to remember also that this is a team effort between parental figures. Perhaps you are not a strong communicator, but your partner is. In that case, your partner might be the one who observes the child's behavior, comes to you to discuss how to handle a situation, and then engages the child in dialogue.

Parenting with others is certainly easier when you agree on style. However, research shows that having at least one authoritative parent is better than having none.

In the past, it was more culturally acceptable for men to take on an authoritarian or disciplinarian role, or for men to feel like that had to be their role. The landscape has shifted in this area with more men feeling comfortable engaging in the nurturing aspects of the authoritative style.

We have emphasized in this book that we are providing a framework with ideas and suggestions, not hard-and-fast rules. This is the closest we come to making a firm recommendation. Based on research from Baumrind and others, as well as my own experience as a child and as a parent, I do believe the authoritative parenting style—with an emphasis on high expectations, high nurturing, and continual two-way communication between parent and child—is the best foundation for raising resilient children.

THE IMPORTANCE OF CONSISTENCY

Consistency comes in many forms and is important for several reasons. One kind of consistency is in expectation. Parents must determine what their expectations for the child are and then clearly communicate them. If rules are constantly shifting, children will not understand what is expected of them. Growing up, our mom set the expectation for us, even when we were small, that we would be respectful of adults and well-behaved in public. If we strayed, there were consequences.

Having expectations already set can be very helpful, especially when you are short on time or energy. Here's a concrete example. With Lena, I have set the expectation with her that when it is time to wrap up a play date, we will get ready to go with minimum fuss. In practice, I always give her a five-minute notice before it is time to go. I set the timer on my phone for five minutes, selecting a loud and peppy ringtone, and I let her watch me start the countdown. I give a one-minute warning, and when the timer goes off, Lena knows that it is time to go. In this way, she has the space to wrap up her playtime in her own way without my interference, but she also knows that my expectation is that when the five minutes are up, playtime is done.

Consistency in implementation is also quite important. Children are smart. They know how to spot inconsistencies and exploit them to their benefit. Every parent has surely heard some version of, "Oh, well Dad said I could have ice cream for dinner." If parents have a difference of opinion on a given standard, it can be difficult to coordinate and present a unified front. Nonetheless, it is important to do so. When parents are not on the same page, it can be problematic in the long run.

In this version of good cop/bad cop, if one parent enforces a rule the way the partners previously agreed, and the other gives in, it can provide fertile ground for resentment to build between the parents. It can also lead the child to develop a negative perspective of the parents, which ultimately can morph into outright disrespect.

If parents are not on the same page in setting and enforcing standards, problems will arise. It is important to take care of disagreement regarding standards in private rather than in front of the child. Similarly, a frustrated parent should try to refrain from disrespectful comments about the other partner in front of the child so as not to undermine their partner's authority.

The final area of consistency to consider is in action. In other words, how do parents behave and how do they expect their children to behave? For example, if parents have a high standard for their child in terms of keeping one's word, but they regularly go back on their own word, problems can arise. Consider the case where a parent says no to some request six times, and on the seventh time, caves in. This sends the message that "no" does not mean "no," and it can embolden the child to pursue a similar strategy whenever she is not getting her way. It can be hard to stick to your guns when you are tired or just running low on patience, but engaging in this form of accommodating behavior can be especially detrimental in the long run.

DETERMINING YOUR NONNEGOTIABLES

Having defined one's style gives parents a springboard to figure out the rules and expectations they will go to bat to enforce, even with family members and others interacting with the child. Monitoring and enforcing nonnegotiables requires a lot of energy, so think carefully about those areas that are most important.

For my friend Robin, no sugar for her children is a nonnegotiable. However, she knows her parents love sweets. And because she wants her kids to be able to spend time with their grandparents, she knows she has to navigate the situation carefully. She invests considerable energy into maintaining this boundary. At her parents' sweets-filled home, she supervises visits, or if she cannot be present and needs babysitting help, she asks her parents to come to her house, where she has more control over the food and drinks on offer. For parents whose children spend a lot of time with grandparents and others, boundary setting is much more important on a day-to-day basis.

Other common areas where parents might draw a red line are around television (types of programs, number of hours, etc.) and time on phones and social media. Another may be around grandparents or family friends bringing toys or treats on every visit. Typically, these boundaries emerge from a deeply held family value, the crossing of which would lessen the value's importance.

One of my mom's guiding principles was around prioritizing education. In looking out over the landscape, she knew we needed access to a diversity of educational opportunities to be best prepared for the future. This often required going outside of our immediate neighborhood for classes and activities.

Starting with Nora, our mom began driving us all over the city for various educational programs. Some family members, including our dad, thought Mom was going to too much trouble. In Dad's mind, he went to neighborhood schools and still went to college and grad school and got a good job. Why couldn't we?

As we got older, our dad thought we should use public transportation to get to our various activities on our own. But conditions had changed from when he was growing up, and public transportation was not always a safe or time-efficient option. Our mom was aware of this reality, but our dad did not think in those terms. So, Mom invested the time and energy into providing us with these opportunities for learning even when others did not completely understand.

NONNEGOTIABLES

During one Christmas season, Nora called to tell me that she asked her little ones to donate their gifts to two or three charities.

I was shocked. Why would my loving daughter choose to do such a thing? Did I overemphasize or incorrectly reinforce the value of being generous and thoughtful of others when my children were growing up? My philosophy regarding altruism versus selfishness was carefully derived from much reading, including several of Ayn Rand's books. Perhaps it was not explained adequately to the children at a stage when they were old enough to understand.

I expressed concerns to my Bible study friends, and some seemed baffled. One lady suggested, "Why don't you just ask your daughter why she chose to do what she did?" I took her advice.

Nora explained that her children usually receive an overabundance of toys and games from friends and relatives. She felt that the feeling of giving is in itself a gift that keeps on giving. She went on to say that the little ones had a lot of fun choosing and wrapping the items that they would donate. In addition, she involved them in delivering the gifts to a nearby children's hospital.

This was still concerning to me, my thought being, "What about the person, like your dad, who gave the gifts while imagining the delight they would bring to the recipients?"

After I shared my perspective, Nora explained that she did give it a lot of thought and came up with what she considered was the best policy for all concerned. Her decision was nonnegotiable.

200 · RAISING GRITTY KIDS

PARENTING IN CONCENTRIC CIRCLES

As discussed in chapter 1, our parenting framework considers the child, with all her individual preferences and characteristics, in the center of the model. Parents form the first circle of influence, followed by progressively distant relationships, like with other family, teachers, community, and finally, the culture at large. In terms of monitoring and enforcing expectations, parents have a certain amount of control with those closest to them: grandparents, aunts and uncles, and friends. However, they do not have as much control with teachers, coaches, and others in the community.

For a single parent, the more positive partners in parenting the better. After a parent comes up with his parenting philosophy, expectations, and nonnegotiables, he can look for people and programs to help carry out the plan.

In the community circles, there may be other outlets parents can explore as unexpected sources of help. Many years ago, my mom had a student whose parents were hearing impaired. This made certain classroom interactions for the child more complicated than for other students. Once Mom better understood the student's home setting, she was able to research and suggest ways to help the student. If you have unique situations at home, look to your circle to provide help where you need it.

It may seem odd to quote Joan Crawford, famously portrayed in the movie *Mommie Dearest* as anything but a model mom. Alas, in her autobiography, she shared a sentiment with which many a working parent can agree:

Often there's no help in the home, but there are neighbors and

PARENTING WITH OTHERS · 201

friends and the people at nurseries and day-care centers. All of them help a child to learn to get along with all sorts of people and become more independent. Seeing people encourages him to make decisions for himself.[37]

When children are school age, they spend a lot of time with their teachers, which unfortunately can have a negative impact if a teacher has unchallenged biases, low expectations, or is otherwise disengaged. One friend made the decision to go the homeschooling route after she found the local school environment detrimental to the self-image and self-esteem of her sons. She shared that she sent energetic, hopeful, curious, and engaged children to school, and they would come home fractured and defeated, day after day. Then it would fall to my friend and her husband to try to repair that damage that was done. Finally, they decided to take their kids out of the school system entirely. For them, preserving the psychological and emotional well-being of their sons was paramount. When the line was repeatedly crossed, they acted.

As we have said, you are not parenting in a vacuum. The choices you make will have reverberations in your interactions with other people. Keep that in mind when establishing standards. Consider how you will handle breakdowns and what battles you are willing to fight and those for which you will take a pass. Remember, too, that your children are always watching. Even when disagreements over parenting style or philosophy crop up, try to navigate the conflict in a way that is respectful and constructive.

As has been shown, there will be times when people in your child's circles of influence do not agree with your parenting standards, and they may voice their opinion. During those times, it is important to share that you are making choices based on your understanding of the landscape and your child, and that you are doing what you believe is best.

Just a few weeks after my thirteenth birthday, my parents let me leave home to attend a residential high school outside of Chicago. Some people in our family and community were frankly surprised that they let me go. After years of watching my mom shuttle us to activities rather than let us take the bus or train, many assumed she was simply overprotective, but that was not the case. When it came time for me to choose high schools, my mom understood the landscape and she knew that, ultimately, I would benefit from the experience of attending this particular academy. She knew me, and she trusted that knowledge in spite of the sometimes loudly dissenting opinions of others.

WHEN BREAKDOWNS HAPPEN

In case any doubt remains, let me say again: breakdowns will happen. Someone with whom you are co-parenting will cross one of your red lines.

When that happens, you need to have a plan. It may start with a conversation, ideally not in front of the child. If that is not an option, engaging in respectful conversation is key. As we have mentioned before, you are modeling behavior you want your child to emulate.

Disagreement, between parents in particular, is a dance that has to be carefully navigated. On the one hand, if you fight fair and in plain sight, you are modeling for the child what healthy disagreement looks like. Having differing viewpoints from those around you is a part of life, and you want your children to develop a tool kit for sharing their perspective and hearing others' in a healthy way.

On the other hand, too much arguing or outright unfair fighting comes with its own problems. Not knowing the full context or relative unimportance of a rift, a child can find the situation disorienting and may interpret an argument as proof that the family fiber is being rent.

It may be almost too obvious to state, but the first act of compromise is to try to speak in terms the other person can understand. For example, my husband spends his spare time reading articles about scientific advances and generally respects conclusions backed by research rather than more anecdotal evidence. When we have a difference of opinion and I want to share my view, oftentimes I will seek out research to back up my perspective. If I cannot find reputable research that bolsters my point, I take it as an indication that I may need to reconsider my position.

While it is important to show consideration for the other person's perspective, you should also lay out why you are embracing a certain standard and share how you would like the issue addressed the next time. It is not enough to say, "Hey, not having the kids eat chocolate is important to me." Explain why and lay out a plan so that breakdowns are less likely to happen again. Perhaps you say, "The next time they come to visit, I would prefer no chocolate. You can give them toast with jam, but no chocolate."

Once you have made the line crystal clear, you have to decide what will happen if it is crossed again, and then follow through.

For example, "As I've said, my preference is that the children not eat chocolate. If it happens again, I will have to be present when we visit because this is a nonnegotiable for me."

Be prepared for potential ramifications if you lay down the law like this. The grands may choose not to watch your children anymore, and it is fully their right, if they feel strongly enough about their opinion on the matter.

In all conversations, make sure you are not coming from a reactionary place. You may feel angry, hurt, or frustrated if your boundaries are being continually tested. But being firm, reasonable, and consistent is generally the best way forward.

IMPORTANCE OF WATERING YOUR FERN

"Ferns are not houseplants that you can forget about and water whenever the hell you remember. If you want a houseplant that you can neglect, I suggest that you grow more plants like Sansevieria."

—RAFFAELE DI LALLO, OHIO TROPICS BLOG

Good advice for fern caretakers, good advice for parents. Having a healthy relationship with your mate—and the other adults involved in parenting your children—makes it easier when those inevitable, tough discussions on boundaries and nonnegotiables do come up. Building healthy relationships requires an ongoing investment of time and energy. Finding commonality, acknowledging contributions, developing strong bonds by moving through challenges together, and sharing and allowing vulnerability: these are all ways to grow the emotional capital between you and others.

Taking time to replenish your stores of goodwill with your mate is very important but is sometimes overlooked in the activity of day-to-day parenting. However, if you find small ways to reinforce positive emotional connection continually between you and others, having tough discussions will be that much easier.

LEANING ON COMMUNITY

Sometimes parents need a helping hand, and this is where community comes in.

Single moms, for example, can find organizations like Becoming a Man or boys' foundations to help find a mentor for a son. A trusted uncle, cousin, or other family member could also be helpful. Any choice should, of course, involve regular parental oversight.

In raising daughters with no brothers, parents might ask uncles or male cousins to tell stories of childhood antics to give girls insight to the male mindset. My brother shared such a story in his weekly newspaper column.

He began with a quote from Paul Laurence Dunbar, "Fur boys is fools an' allus was,"[38] and went on to describe a boyhood experience. Having received a brand-new BB gun for Christmas, he was excited to see exactly how far away a BB could travel and hit a target. He went outside just in time to see his older sister at the end of the block as she was on her way to visit a neighbor.

Taking careful aim at her backside, he fired. Fortunately, he missed. Still, he got an angry lecture from Mom telling him the nature of the pain and suffering he could have caused. She made him turn over the BB gun and told him to expect a good spanking when Dad got home from work.

Although he was sorry for what he had done, waiting more than two hours for a whupping seemed like cruel and unusual punishment.

I leaned on community when Kara's grandmother helped to make the majorette uniforms for the parades in which Kara and her sister twirled baton. She made delightful Halloween costumes as well.

One of my aunts was part of our extended parenting family when I was a child. She and my mom were alike in many ways. Both were very attractive young ladies who wore the latest fashions, and as career women, always dressed appropriately for their professions. Mom was a nurse. My aunt was an administrative assistant. Their difference interestingly had to do with their comfort in discussing bodily functions.

Ironically, my mom, the OB/GYN nurse who knew a lot about the human body, was prudish. As youngsters, we never heard anything about "unmentionables" from her. On the other hand, my aunt was quite carefree and rather matter-of-fact about such matters.

In our house, we never discussed sex. Still, as kids, we were really curious about what our mom and dad "did." One Sunday, when we had company over for a visit, everyone was sitting in the living room enjoying good conversation when my brother noticed our father send a signal to our mom. It was a secret wink or maybe a come-hither smile. Anyway, she got up and went down the hall to the master bedroom. Dad sat for a minute or two, commented on something someone said, then excused himself, got up and headed for the master bedroom. My brother signaled to me and my sister that we should go and investigate. Nobody would notice our absence because the adults in the room were engrossed in conversation.

We slowly and quietly inched toward the bedroom door. First, we placed an ear to it. We couldn't hear anything. Back in the day, some doors locked with skeleton keys and therefore had a keyhole. This one did. My brother squinched and tried to see through the tiny opening. He pulled away and gestured for me to try. Nothing remarkable. So, we went back into the living room.

When our parents returned to join the guests, we quickly went to examine the room to see if we could find any clues, but we found nothing. We never learned at home what could have been going on in that bedroom.

Now, my aunt was much more straightforward. As we each entered puberty, she was the one who explained the changes in our bodies. She was the one who asked my sister and me to come closer when small bumps could be seen through our undershirts, to see if we were beginning to develop breasts. She was the one who explained how to take care of other unexpected events on the horizon. She tried not to embarrass us, but of course we were both embarrassed and glad to know. After all, we were first and foremost our mother's children and had internalized her attitude about modesty. Also, our aunt was the one who described teenaged crushes as the tingle in a certain part of the body, and she wasn't talking about the heart.

It was a good thing to have an aunt willing to share a slightly different point of view, because changes in the physical body can be kind of scary to a preteen.

Without a doubt, extending the parenting community is a good thing to do. There are many resources available. Parents certainly can't do everything. We have already mentioned how mentors can be found at museums. Other organizations can be involved too. Through a church program, Nora participated in a building project in Mexico and David participated in Habitat for Humanity. Not only did these experiences provide a way to express an interest in social justice, but practical skills were learned as well.

People who have similar interests to a child can be a wonderful resource. A grandparent may be the one to help a child learn fishing or hunting skills. My uncle, a professional guide and fisherman in Florida, taught me fishing and boating as a teen. An aunt or uncle who loves to golf might share this passion.

Early on, my oldest daughter exhibited traits more compatible with those of my younger sister, whom my daughter admired very much. It was fortunate the two could spend some time together, and it was great for me to be able to go to this sister for advice on my daughter's behavior and choices that were perfectly acceptable, but did not conform to my own.

My older sister proved to be helpful in sharing some of the trials and woes of growing up exceptionally brilliant. At one point she shared that it might have been helpful for her own socioemotional development if she had gone to a secondary school with other intellectually gifted students. This information helped, and when Kara had an opportunity to attend such a school at two years younger than her classmates, the decision was easier to make.

· ·

As a parent, if you know your child and yourself, you may realize there are areas where you need help or where a member of your community can provide insight or support that you cannot. As they say, it takes a village to produce productive, well-balanced, resilient members of society.

In elementary school, I had a wonderful art teacher who unexpectedly took me under her wing. I was at once plump and awkward and adventurous and longing to experience more of the world. Mrs. M introduced our fourth-grade class to calligraphy, origami, and other arts that required patience and exacting precision. I greatly admired her discerning taste

PARENTING WITH OTHERS · 209

and deep appreciation for a job well done. Always dressed impeccably and with incredible flair, she was by far the most glamorous teacher at my school. And she had interesting friends and a talented artist husband. Sensing my thirst for experiences beyond what I had been exposed to thus far, my mom encouraged my relationship with Mrs. M.

We stayed in touch for many years after. When I graduated from high school, she took me for a celebratory lunch and presented me with a beautiful antique, embroidered handkerchief. It felt like an acknowledgment that I was on my way to new adventures and social circles.

Aside from befriending me, Mrs. M gave me a taste for what was possible in my future. She was an African-American woman operating in a more integrated environment, which was not typical at that time, certainly not in Chicago. In addition, one of her two accomplished sons had moved to Spain to work in corporate finance. Most people I knew were comfortable staying right where they were and saw no reason to do things differently. For me, the prospect of living abroad, and working in finance at that, was absolutely intoxicating.

Mrs. M influenced my life in meaningful ways. Be on the lookout for such individuals, kindred spirits who elicit a spark in your child that you may not have seen before.

"People say it takes a village to raise a child. People ask me how my daughter is doing. She's only doing good if your daughter's doing good. We're all one family. We have the ability to approach our race like ants, or we have the ability to approach our race like crabs."

—KANYE WEST

PARENTING WITH OTHERS TOOL KIT

As we have said, no one parents in a vacuum. Grandparents, extended family, teachers, coaches, and members of the community interact with your child on a daily basis. Here are some ideas for parenting with others most effectively.

DO A PARENTING PHILOSOPHY INVENTORY WITH YOUR PARTNER

Revisit the parenting philosophies presented earlier in this chapter. Think about how each of you naturally approaches parenting, where you complement each other, and where you clash. If you want to shift from one style to another, think of how your partner can support you in that effort. Identify areas of potential conflict, say differences in philosophies on extracurricular activities—which ones to pursue, and how much time and money you will commit. Memorialize this inventory in a written fashion, actually writing down with pen and paper the strengths you each bring, the challenges you might face in co-parenting, and how you will tackle future disagreements.

THINK ABOUT AND DOCUMENT NONNEGOTIABLES

This is something to do individually and then come together with your partner to discuss. Think through those areas you feel very strongly about, as well as those you feel strongly about but would be more willing to negotiate on. For instance, a nonnegotiable might be to not have your child participate in unfamiliar research studies.

After you have written your lists, come up with a plan for how to navigate each one, particularly in areas where these might be in conflict with others in your larger parenting community.

CHECK OUT *FATHERLY*

This is a recommendation for moms and dads alike. The creators of the *Fatherly* newsletter and website (https://www.fatherly.com/) do a great job of encouraging parents and dads in particular to embrace a model of parenting that is more aligned with the authoritative style, which is most correlated with raising resilient children. If you happen to be a mom reading this book, steer Dad to check it out.

DEVELOP RULES OF ENGAGEMENT

With your partner, develop a set of guidelines to govern disagreements. These rules could include things like, "We agree to be on the same page in front of the children and resolve our differences later" or "It's okay to disagree in front of the children, but we will be respectful and fair in how we do it." Keep in mind that your rules of engagement can depend on the situation and may evolve over time as the child grows in emotional maturity.

· ·

THE AMERICAN EXPERIMENT

In a way, my parenting style evolved because the country itself was shifting and changing as it sought to survive, thrive, and live up to its original ideals. Think about it. When the Statue of Liberty was conceived, the issues of the Civil War were still very much in the air. At the time it was completed and delivered to the United States, women still had no right to vote, child labor was exploited, and African-Americans, having recently gained freedoms, saw them wiped out. Some adjustments needed to happen.

In my opinion, the freedom to change requires a degree of autonomy and is one reason the cautionary advice to not lose oneself in parenting

212 · RAISING GRITTY KIDS

is significant. As a working mom, having my own source of income made it possible for me to not compromise when my parenting ideals did not agree with my husband's.

Let me be more specific. My husband and I disagreed on the issue of schooling. On more than one occasion, he could have persuaded me to lean in his direction by simply not providing funds. Because I had some degree of autonomy, however, this didn't happen. Having the funds and a car made it possible for me to forge ahead with my plan.

Sometimes my husband and I visited a favorite breakfast spot, where good conversation helped to bridge the gap in our different parenting outlooks. As we talked, I realized that he wasn't vehemently opposed to my schooling idea. Rather, he thought that whatever happened for him as a child was probably good enough for his kids.

When two different personalities and backgrounds or perspectives come together in marriage, there will inevitably be differences of opinion. At some point, something has to give when two perfectly legitimate perspectives clash. Smoothing things over may involve participating more in something your mate enjoys.

With grandparents, a generation gap might contribute to a difference of opinion regarding parenting decisions. My strategy was to explain my thinking and often back it up with an invitation to experience the landscape we were trying to navigate with our children. This happened when Kara expressed an interest in playing in the Chicago Youth Symphony Orchestra. Some family members did not get it. Interestingly, as my mother learned more, she became a dedicated advocate for Kara and also volunteered with other young adults interested in music.

• •

PARENTING WITH OTHERS · 213

REACH OUT

At the beginning of the chapter, Duchess Kate Middleton is quoted as saying that asking for help should not be a sign of weakness. In that same talk, the Duchess goes on to say, "Personally, becoming a mother has been such a rewarding and wonderful experience. However, at times it has also been a huge challenge—even for me who has support at home that most mothers do not."[39]

If someone with the resources and assistance of the presumptive future Queen of England finds motherhood at times challenging to navigate, so much more the case for the rest of us.

If you see personality traits in your child that you do not understand or if you see that your child needs support someone else can provide, reach out to your circle. The ultimate goal is raising resilient children, and it takes a clear parenting philosophy, partners on the same page, and a supportive community, whatever form that takes.

The next chapter discusses the process of launching into the real world.

CHAPTER 11

Ready to Launch

"The child has shown us the basic principle underlying the process of education, which he has expressed in the words, 'Teach me to do things by myself.' ...The adult must help the child do things entirely on his own. For if the child does not reach the point of ceasing to rely on the help of adults and becoming independent, he will never fully mature intellectually or morally."

—MARIA MONTESSORI, *EDUCATION AND PEACE*

PARTIAL LAUNCH

This business of launching could best be described as a process, not a single event. Not all children are ready to launch at the same developmental stage. Launching may occur much earlier or later than expected. It may happen in some areas of life, but not in others.

Kara was ready to leave home early. At age nine, she asked me if she could get a GED! At age eleven, she heard about a residential high school and asked about applying. She was known to be a responsible risk taker who thrived on challenges. It was a difficult decision. Despite one teacher's admonition that her socioemotional development would possibly suffer and at some point her psycho-intellectual development might be compromised, Kara skipped fifth grade. Though Kara clearly demonstrated a degree of maturity beyond her years, I did not totally disregard the teacher's viewpoint. Attending this residential high school would mean skipping another grade, starting as a sophomore at the age of thirteen.

Choosing the math and science academy wasn't perfect in every way, but it turned out to be a blessing. Kara found lots of peers with similar interests. One moment in time stands out. It was fall of her first year. Kara called home one evening at about 7:00 p.m. Was she homesick? Not exactly.

"Mom, guess what!? We're going to have a party. And we're going to order pizza..." My immediate thought was "A party on a Wednesday night? Was this choice a mistake?" Then Kara finished her sentence: "and do problem sets!" You can imagine my sigh of relief. I had been a witness to her delight in solving math problems. She continued to be rather unique in her love of physics as well, but that was okay at a math and science academy.

At one point, Kara was interviewed by a journalist who wanted to write about the difference in learning styles between boys and girls in physics classes. She ended up on the cover of a national news magazine that featured the article. In another school setting, Kara might have been taunted as a nerd, which can be damaging to a child's self-concept. Instead, Kara received "Way to go!" approval from fellow students at school. The success of a launch can depend to some extent on the nature of obstacles confronted in the process.

Taking into account the words of the fifth-grade teacher who cautioned about Kara's socioemotional development, I brought her home each

216 · RAISING GRITTY KIDS

Friday evening and returned her to school on Sunday. This was an option, although most students remained on campus throughout the weekend. In a sense, this represented a partial launch, with ongoing parental oversight. I knew my child, and this seemed to be the best of both worlds.

. . . .

From the time their children are born, parents know these little humans will eventually launch into adulthood. What that looks like, when it happens, and what ongoing supports are provided varies from family to family. In this chapter, we will discuss steps you can take now with young children to get them ready for that eventuality.

WHAT DOES LAUNCHING LOOK LIKE TO YOU?

Launching is complicated. It is different for each parent and child. As my mom's story shows, I was ready to leave home early, heading off to high school at thirteen and to Harvard University shortly after turning sixteen. However, after some questionable choices, I returned home in my midtwenties for just under a year, humbled and chastened, in order to regroup and get back on track. My parents were fine with that, but some parents might have said, "No, don't come back here." Some parents do not want their children to move away at all. And still others expect their children to leave but ultimately come back at some point to help take care of them.

So, what does launching look like to you? Does it mean that your child will be self-sufficient and not need monetary support? Do you have expectations around emotional and psychological self-reliance? Some parents view having a job that pays for all living expenses as a successful launch.

READY TO LAUNCH · 217

Others encourage their children to pursue particular career paths, such as becoming a doctor, lawyer, or engineer, and see anything different as suboptimal. Sometimes parents encourage the child to go for their passion and might even provide support to that end. Some have a desire to see their children contributing to society and giving back.

Knowing things may change as your child reveals herself and her particular makeup, you must first settle the question of what launching looks like.

PROPS

If your child is still in diapers or even elementary school, you may think it is too early to start envisioning an eventual launch into adulthood. In actuality, the process starts at birth and continues until the child leaves home.

Different parents may offer different kinds of support, and even those may change over time. Some parents offer support through college and beyond. Some stop the day a child turns eighteen. The following provides food for thought as you consider and discuss with your partner.

COMMUNITY/EDUCATION

When deciding where to live, many parents look for neighborhoods with the best school systems. This is one type of planning for the future. One article, about the lengths to which some parents will go, says, "The frenzy over getting children into elite New York preschools is well documented. Parents sweat, barter and bribe to get their 4-year-olds into prestigious early education programs...there's the implicit belief that a premier prekindergarten program guarantees an early leg up in a nearly 14-year battle to gain admission to the country's most competitive colleges."[40] In choosing a neighborhood, parents are putting networks beyond educational ones in place. As mentioned in chapter 1, the community in which you primarily operate helps to define your child's horizon of possibility, which in turn impacts the choices he will have available down the road.

FINANCIAL

A big support parents offer is financial, and again, how long parents offer that support varies. My grandmother insisted that my mom and her siblings contribute to rent and household expenses as soon as they could get a job. There was no discussion involved. It was simply expected. When my mom got her first job at fifteen, she gave a percentage of her income for household expenses. My mom has said that this experience cemented the idea that it takes money to live in this world.

Here are some questions to consider related to money and finances:

- How much would you like to contribute to your child's education?
- What will your child be required to contribute in terms of scholarships, grants, or part-time and summer work?
- When will your child be required to get her first job?
- What bills will she be required to pay and starting at what age?
- Are there other financial gifts you would like to pass along, for example, a down payment for a first house or seed money to open a business?

There is no right or wrong answer to these questions. The point is to start thinking about your family's situation. I have a friend whose parents paid for her education through medical school because they wanted her not to be burdened by school debt. Some parents, on the other hand, believe it is a formative experience for the child to figure out how to pay for school.

Keep in mind that one of the root causes of income and net worth inequality in America is that some children have a generational safety net to rely on while others do not. You have to determine what is most important to you. However, if you decide you want to provide money toward college, property, or a business, for example, and you start saving and investing consistently each month from when the child is small, you could have a nice gift by the time he is eighteen or twenty-one. That can be a real game changer, something to lean on in uncertain times.

"You should leave your children enough so they can do anything, but not enough so they can do nothing."

—WARREN BUFFETT

NETWORKS

When we were young, my siblings and I went to our dad's job to learn what his work entailed. For nearly forty years, he worked in the filming and production of local Chicago news. It was always tremendously exciting to visit the studio, glamorous and mysterious and filled with local celebrities. As mentioned earlier, letting children observe their parents' work life helps them see the parent as a whole person with a job and colleagues, challenges and responsibilities. On another level, it provides children with their first concept of a career network.

One college scholarship that David won came after our father's colleague suggested applying and wrote a letter of recommendation. When I was in college, I landed an interview at the Chicago Board of Trade for a summer job because our next-door neighbor held a seat on the exchange and knew who was hiring. Having a robust network provides a resiliency advantage because one never knows what connection may ultimately lead to an unexpected opportunity. Arming your children with the seeds of a network early, and emphasizing the importance of cultivating such a network, can be very valuable.

HOBBIES AND AVOCATIONS

Involving your child in sports, music, art, and other activities is important to establish and provide connections outside of immediate family and friends. For example, some of my childhood music friends have gone on to illustrious careers. One even played at the 2009 presidential inauguration. I have been fortunate because of these connections to visit backstage occasionally to meet other classical music superstars.

Hobbies and passions can provide other opportunities down the road. Sports is the classic example where an interviewer and candidate might bond over having played the same game in high school or college. Justified or not, the reality is that hiring decisions often hinge more on affinity than meritocratic reasons alone. You give your child a leg up when she has a potential point of connection with future interviewers.

EXPOSURE TO LANGUAGES

Like hobbies and avocations, learning other languages can pay dividends down the road. This is a support you can provide when your child is young, long before she has to take a language in middle or high school.

One of my friends has his children studying Mandarin, and their family takes trips to China regularly so the children can practice. Now that they are older, he is making plans to have them attend summer camp in China.

My sister studied Russian, and my brother and I both studied Japanese. At the time, each of these language choices made sense because of foreign relations between the United States and these countries. Since then, the landscape has changed and knowing other languages might be more relevant. Regardless, the process of learning a language provides cognitive benefits, including improved problem-solving and critical-thinking skills, better ability to concentrate and multitask, and better listening skills. Furthermore, bilingual and multilingual people switch between tasks and monitor changes in the environment more easily.[41] All of these skills are useful for navigating changing landscapes.

MINI LAUNCHES

With an eye toward an eventual launch into adulthood, one key strategy parents can implement early is what my mom calls *mini launches*. These are organically occurring situations where the child is given more autonomy to practice decision-making.

These should be situations where children can truly make a

choice and deal with the consequences, positive or negative. Of course, these should never put the child in danger or result in an irreversible outcome. If the result is favorable, the child can enjoy the reward. If not, she can learn from her choice in order to choose differently next time. Both are instructive.

Years back, on a steamy summer day, I saw a dad walking with a toddler decked out in a frilly dress and tiny, heavy rain boots. They looked terribly hot, but she looked pleased with her sartorial selection.

Here are a few examples where young children could be given a choice to develop autonomy:

- Selecting clothing for the day
- Deciding on a weekend activity
- Choosing a go-away or summer camp, or choosing not to attend
- Choosing books at the library (here parents also gain a sense of the child's interests, a way to know the child)
- Suggesting what to cook with Dad or bake with Mom
- Choosing what to eat at dinner from the available options

Incorporate the mini launches that are most aligned with your parenting style and that of your partner.

With some decisions, parents have to determine their overarching priorities. For example, are you willing to do all the housework so your child can focus solely on academics and extracurriculars? Or is this an opportunity to start teaching how to balance time between work (in this case, school) and other responsibilities?

READY TO LAUNCH · 223

Another area of focus should be around peer pressure. To be ready to launch, children need to know how to respond in these situations. The mini launches, which parents design, can help ground the child's character around family and individual values. A child who knows what she stands for is much more likely to withstand peer pressure. For the young child, this might look like the parent not intervening or mediating in every dispute between siblings or with friends.

Here again, open communication between parent and child is important. The child should feel comfortable going to the parents to talk about peer pressure. Parents can give an adult's perspective on how to interpret the situation and some suggestions on how to handle it. Developing internal fortitude is a key component of resilience. It enables children to stand up for what they believe in despite outside pressure.

HOW ARE YOU PLANNING TODAY?

Preparing for a child's launch into adulthood does not happen overnight. It takes time to develop the decision-making and other skills being honed through mini launches. The important thing is to provide opportunities in everyday situations for your child to interact with others, make choices, persevere through challenges, and grow into ever-increasing responsibility.

If you are planning to provide some form of financial support down the road, starting early will make it easier and less painful. If you invest small sums of money on a regular basis when your child is a baby and continue doing so until he turns eighteen, you can take full advantage of the power of compounding. Vanguard, the well-respected investment adviser, provides this example:

Let's say you start saving for college when your child is born. You invest in an account and save $25 a week for the first 9 years of his or her life but then stop—for a total investment of $11,700. If your account earns 6% a year, you'll have about $26,750 at the end of 18 years.

Now let's say you wait 9 years before you start to save, and then save the same $25 per week until your child is 18. Factoring in the $11,700 investment and 6% return, you'll have accumulated about $15,800 by the time he or she goes off to college.

As you can see, you'll earn almost $11,000 more for college in the first scenario, thanks to the power of compounding![42]

If you are reading this and have not started planning financially or otherwise, that is okay. It is never too late. Start where you are. Better to begin now than not at all.

LAUNCHING IS A BALANCING ACT

As parents plan these mini launches, they should ensure it is always in a safe environment. Failures should not be dangerous or devastating. The balancing act comes in knowing how far to let the child fail, in what areas, and when to intervene. Parents need not make hard-and-fast rules in this regard. However, they have to understand the child, her strengths and interests, as well as the challenges the situation presents.

Heightened vigilance is required at certain points of development. For example, toddlers who do not know any better routinely test boundaries, and teenagers whose brains are still developing are notorious for exhibiting questionable judgment. With teens in particular, you may want to provide

READY TO LAUNCH · 225

perspective on how a particular action could have long-lasting, even permanent, impact.

One factor that figures into this balancing act is the child's risk tolerance. I was always somewhat risk loving. At age eleven, I was ready to see the world and preparing for a trip to Russia—without my parents—as part of a youth orchestra. At twelve, I was already plotting how I could leave the confines of our quiet neighborhood to attend a residential high school. My brother, on the other hand, was perfectly content to stay close to home. He did travel, but somewhat reluctantly, and he always expressed his preference to stay put in Chicago.

NOT READY TO LAUNCH

Even when it was time for college, my brother was not interested in going away. Mom was a little worried when David said, "I'll just stay home and go to the college down the street." She wondered if this was going to be a forever thing, that David was not going to leave home without some prodding.

Because of trust developed over the years, our mom could speak frankly with David to find out what he was thinking. She learned that he preferred to pay for college on his own and one way to make that happen was to stay home and attend a local school. Still, our mom asked him to consider more than the cost and to think of which schools would be best aligned with his interests and career goals. Ultimately, David decided to attend the Illinois Institute of Technology. He applied for and won several scholarships. He also got a part-time job on campus, which alleviated his concern about affording it. After a year of commuting to campus, he also ended up leaving home to live in his fraternity's house.

One sign that your child might not be ready to launch is a failure to follow through on things. Life is full of mundane but necessary activities like going to work, paying bills, doing the laundry, and on and on. If your child is not showing commitment to push through these mundane tasks, she may not be ready to launch. If you notice this tendency in your child, take a step back and consider whether something has happened to cause this outcome.

Ask questions to determine the root cause and find ways to encourage the behavior you would like to see. Engaging in activities that require patience and perseverance develops a form of mental grit that can be applied across many practical domains.

Finally, failure in life is inevitable. Learning to contextualize it and recover is an important skill for long-term success. Being able to bounce back from mistakes is in some ways the true indication of a resilient character. When your child is able to try, fail, dust himself off, and try again, you can feel confident that he will be up to life's future challenges. Again, if you are not seeing these behaviors, do not be afraid to step back, reassess, and look for new opportunities to help your child develop along these lines.

READY-TO-LAUNCH TOOL KIT

In a way, this entire chapter is your tool kit. We are asking you to think about what launching looks like for you, what supports you want to provide, and how long you will provide these supports. Here are some other specific actions you can take to help you and your child prepare for the day when they strike out on their own.

DEVELOP A READY-TO-LAUNCH FINANCIAL PLAN

When it comes to saving and investing for your child's future, the advice is varied and depends on your particular situation and goals. There are many excellent books and resources online geared specifically around financial planning for parents. If saving for college is a priority, you might consider tax-advantaged accounts like 529 plans or custodial IRAs.

MAKE A WILL AND ESTATE PLAN

No one wants to dwell on what happens if they are no longer able to raise their children, through death or incapacitation. However, this is an important consideration. You can make your wishes known around inheritance (at what age and with what restrictions) and guardianship (legal, financial, or otherwise). An attorney who specializes in estate planning will help you consider your options and draft all relevant paperwork. You may also consider capturing your values, hopes, and expectations for your child in case you are not able to share them yourself. Finally, if you do not already have life insurance separate from your employer, consider buying coverage for you and your partner to help alleviate any financial burden.

HAVE CANDID DISCUSSIONS WITH YOUR CHILD

We have noted in previous chapters how important it is to set clear expectations with your child. This applies equally around the idea of launching into adulthood. If your preference is to have your child leave home at eighteen for good, make that clear. If you want her to work a summer job and contribute money toward household expenses, let her know. If you expect him to pay for college all on his own, set that expectation early. By sharing your views about what launching

228 · RAISING GRITTY KIDS

looks like long before the day arrives, you and your child can talk about how to make it happen.

Now that we've talked about your child and how to prepare her for a future that is filled with uncertainty, let's conclude by talking about you and your role on the journey.

Conclusion

READY TO LAUNCH FOR PARENTS

"If the day ever came, when we were able to accept ourselves and our children exactly as we and they are, then I believe we would have come very close to an ultimate understanding of what 'good parenting' means."

—FRED ROGERS, *MISTER ROGERS TALKS WITH PARENTS*

In an article for the *Huffington Post*, Brené Brown shares what she calls "The Wholehearted Parenting Manifesto."[43] Much like we encouraged you to do in chapter 10, Brown stepped back and thought through her parenting philosophy, who she was being as a parent, what expectations she had for her children, and how she wanted her children to walk in this world. Then, she memorialized it in a statement addressed to her children.

We recommend that you take time to read Brown's post and manifesto, and then consider writing your own based on what you have gleaned from this book, the questions you have been asking yourself, and the self-reflection you have been doing as a parent.

Even if you never pick up this book again, you will have your parenting manifesto for reference, a document of your guiding principles, your North Star, as it were.

YOU CAN DO IT

In writing this book I wanted to take my mom's wisdom and crystalize my own thinking about how her organic parenting style could be used to navigate these uncertain times. I wanted to alleviate my own anxieties around parenting and to provide a resource for others to do the same.

For those who want the "too long; didn't read" version, here is a quick recap of the main ideas from our organic parenting framework:

- Remember the crocodile. Look out over the shifting landscape and consider what is coming. Let this understanding guide the parenting decisions you make today so you can best prepare your child for the uncertain future that lies ahead.
- Be responsive. No one gets parenting right 100 percent of the time, but if you can inch closer to that "just right" style, balancing high demandingness with high responsiveness and open communication, then you are moving in the right direction.
- Know your child. Each child has a unique combination of preferences, interests, personality traits, strengths, and weaknesses. Give your child the tools she needs to develop her interests, appreciate her physical presence, embrace her social landscape, practice self-compassion and emotional resilience, and develop her unique spirituality and ethical grounding.

232 · RAISING GRITTY KIDS

- Use money as a tool. Look for ways to organically talk about money with your child, removing the emotion and anxiety that often surrounds it. Help your child use money as a tool to facilitate pursuit of his goals and in support of his values.
- Don't lose yourself. Though you may feel selfish about taking time for yourself, you are truly helping your child, as well as yourself, if you do. Foster friendships, rekindle interests, and participate in hobbies apart from your child.
- Determine your philosophy. This conversation should take place in conjunction with your partner, so that you present a united front to your child. Talk to those in your child's outer social circles, both as reinforcers of your nonnegotiables and as sources of support.
- Prepare mini launches: Start helping your child prepare for his eventual launch with ongoing practice in a safe environment.

You can do this parenting thing. The fact that you picked up this book means you are doing it. You are raising children that will thrive and contribute, laugh and love, and make the world more wondrous for having been a part of it. We want to thank you for your role in shepherding this generation of beautiful souls as they grow and pursue their dreams and passions.

Acknowledgments

I would like to thank my many supportive family members and friends, without whom I might not have dared to attempt this book.

Thank you to my coauthor, and mom extraordinaire, who generously put in oodles of hours to see this project through to completion. I hope you are pleased with the final product! Thank you to you and Dad for all the sacrifices over the years that enabled me to pursue my many fantastic dreams.

Thank you to Tom, for always being up for my next big adventure, for helping to get our little one off to bed on the many nights I was working on the book, and for keeping me well stocked with pretzel sticks and apples. To all my in-laws, who from day one welcomed me into their family with generosity and love.

Thank you to my brother and sister, who were willing to star in this book and who supported the endeavor from start to finish. Your humor and grace in the world are forever an inspiration.

To the others who kindly read through draft versions of anecdotes and whole chapters, gave candid feedback and deserved criticism, weighed in on iterations of cover design and more—Primus, Jonathan, Jessica, Shannon, Beverly, and Janice. I appreciate it so.

To my friends who have been an ongoing source of wisdom and encouragement—Erlinda, Pooja, and Daria. You have inspired me to show up in the world and not be afraid to share my perspectives.

And finally, to the entire Scribe team, who shepherded this project from conception to completion. To Kayla and Barbara, who helped me get crystal clear about what this book was not. To Maggie, whose enthusiasm carried me through many moments of doubt. To Rachael and Cristina and their teams, who patiently worked through multiple iterations of cover copy and design to bring our vision to life.

And to Gail. What can I say…2020 has been a whirlwind, but it would not have been the same without our near-weekly calls to work on this book. I am grateful for your generous listening, for your wise counsel, for how beautifully you captured our voices and helped us to bring this book into the world. Here's to the next book, or five. Onward and upward!

About the Authors

KARA YOKLEY is a data science entrepreneur who balances motherhood and career. She lives by the principles of adaptability, resilience, and the enduring curiosity encouraged by her mother and coauthor, Constance. Kara holds a bachelor's degree in applied mathematics with economics from Harvard College and an MBA in finance from the Wharton School.

CONSTANCE YOKLEY has a bachelor's degree in psychology and math and a master's degree in math education. She has worked as a mentor to exceptional learners for more than twenty years. Her successful parent-child educational programs have been incorporated into curricula across the country.

Notes

1   Brown, Brené. 2012. "The Wholehearted Parenting Manifesto," *HuffPost: The Blog*, September 28, 2012, updated November 28, 2012, Accessed March 23, 2020. https://www.huffpost.com/entry/wholehearted-parenting-manifesto_b_1923011.

2   Suzuki, Shinichi. 2013. *Nurtured by Love*. Translated by Kyoko Selden with Lili Selden. Van Nuys, CA: Alfred Music Publishing. Kindle edition.

3   Megginson, Leon. 1963. "Lessons from Europe for American Business," *Southwestern Social Science Quarterly* 44(1): 3–13, p. 4.

4   Darwin Correspondence Project. n.d. University of Cambridge. Accessed July 28, 2020. https://www.darwinproject.ac.uk/people/about-darwin/six-things-darwin-never-said/evolution-misquotation.

5   Klein, Ezra and Raj Chetty. 2019. "You Have a Better Chance of Achieving 'the American Dream' in Canada Than in America." Vox.com. August 15, 2020. Accessed March 25, 2020. https://www.vox.com/2019/8/15/20801907/raj-chetty-ezra-klein-social-mobility-opportunity.

6   Klein and Chetty, "You Have a Better Chance of Achieving 'the American Dream' in Canada Than in America."

7   Fullerton, Anna M. 1895. *A Handbook of Obstetric Nursing*. Philadelphia: P. Blakiston's Son & Co, p. 173.

8   Watson, John. 1972 (c1928). *Psychological Care of Infant and Child*. New York: Arno Press, p. 81.

9   Roosevelt, Eleanor. 1958 (c1937). *The Autobiography of Eleanor Roosevelt*. New York: Harper & Brothers Publishers, p. 60.

10   Divecha, Diana. 2018. "Why Attachment Parenting Is Not the Same as Secure Attachment." *Great Good Magazine*. May 2. Accessed April 3, 2020. https://greatergood.berkeley.edu/article/item/why_attachment_parenting_is_not_the_same_as_secure_attachment.

11   Benjamin Spock. 1946. *The Common Sense Book of Baby and Child Care*. New York: Duell, Sloan, and Pearce, p. 3.

12   Sample, Ian. 2006. "The Great Man's Answer to the Question of Human Survival: Er, I don't know." *The Guardian*, August 3, 2006. https://www.theguardian.com/science/2006/aug/03/scientists.spaceexploration.

13   Rushing, Helen. 2012. *My World: A Collection of Poems and Short Stories*. Chicago: Heavenly Enterprises Midwest, pp. 50–51.

14   Farnam Street. n.d. "Mental Models: The Best Way to Make Intelligent Decisions (109 Models Explained)." Accessed April 3, 2020. https://fs.blog/mental-models/.

15   Carroll, Lewis (1991) [1871]. "2: The Garden of Live Flowers." *Through the Looking-Glass* (The Millennium Fulcrum Edition 1.7 ed.). Project Gutenberg, retrieved September 9, 2020. https://www.gutenberg.org/files/12/12-h/12-h.htm.

16   Montessori, Maria. 1978. *The Absorbent Mind*. Translated by Claude A. Claremont. New York: Dell Publishing, p. 276.

17   Locke, Judith Y., Marilyn A. Campbell, and David Kavanagh. 2012. "Can a Parent Do Too Much for Their Child? An Examination by Parenting Professionals of the Concept of Overparenting." *Australian Journal of Guidance and Counselling* 22(2): 249–265.

18   Montessori, Maria. 1961. *What You Should Know About Your Child*. Translated by A. Gnana Prakasam. Madras: Kalakshetra Press, p. 15.

19   Suzuki, Shinichi. n.d. Accessed March 25, 2020. https://suzukiassociation.org/.

20   Rushing, Helen. 2012. *My World: A Collection of Poems and Short Stories*. Chicago: Heavenly Enterprises Midwest, pp. 22–23.

21   Grabmeier, Jeff. 2019. "The Importance of Reading to Kids Daily." *The Ohio State University College of Education and Human Ecology News*, April 9, 2019. https://ehe.osu.edu/news/listing/importance-reading-kids-daily-0/.

22   Montessori, Maria. 1978. *The Absorbent Mind*. Translated by Claude A. Claremont. New York: Dell Publishing, p. 27.

23   Julian, Kate. 2020. "Childhood in an Anxious Age." *Atlantic*, May 2020. https://www.theatlantic.com/magazine/archive/2020/05/childhood-in-an-anxious-age/609079/.

24   The Center for Parenting Education. n.d. "Responsibility and Chores," https://centerforparentingeducation.org/library-of-articles/responsibility-and-chores/part-i-benefits-of-chores/.

25 Pinsker, Joe. 2018. "The Way American Parents Think About Chores Is Bizarre." *Atlantic*, December 26, 2018. https://www.theatlantic.com/family/archive/2018/12/allowance-kids-chores-help/578848/.

26 Hoffower, Hillary. 2018. "Paying Kids for Doing Chores Could Teach Them to Be Entitled Rather Than Helpful, Says a Professor Who Studies Wealthy Inequality." *Business Insider*, December 26, 2018. https://www.businessinsider.com/paying-kids-for-chores-allowances-entitlement-2018-12.

27 Doucleff, Michaeleen. 2018. "How to Get Your Kids to Do Chores (Without Resenting It)." *NPR Weekend Edition*, June 9, 2018. https://www.npr.org/sections/goatsandsoda/2018/06/09/616928895/how-to-get-your-kids-to-do-chores-without-resenting-it.

28 Martin, Gary. n.d. "The Phrase Finder." Phrases.org.uk. Retrieved September 30, 2020.

29 Tocqueville, Alexis de. 2013. *Democracy in America*. www.gutenberg.org. Accessed October 6, 2020. https://www.gutenberg.org/files/816/816-h/816-h.htm#link2HCH0002.

30 Hughes, Langston. 1990. "Harlem." Accessed October 15, 2020. https://www.poetryfoundation.org/poems/46548/harlem.

31 Coelho, Paulo. 2003. *Warrior of the Light: A Manual*. Translated by Margaret Jull Costa. New York: HarperCollins Publishers Inc., p. 5.

32 Miller, Lisa. 2015. "What Does It Mean to Raise a Spiritual Child?" Interview by Robin Young. *Here & Now*, WBUR, October 1, 2015. Audio, 11:21. https://www.wbur.org/hereandnow/2015/10/01/spiritual-children-lisa-miller.

33 Pew Research Center. 2014. "2014 Religious Landscape Study, Conducted June 4–September 30, 2014." Accessed October 5, 2020. https://www.pewforum.org/2015/11/03/u-s-public-becoming-less-religious/.

34 Pew Research Center, "2014 Religious Landscape Study."

35 Lary, Banning Kent. 2015. "Perceptions of Empty Nest Mothers from Diverse Socioeconomic Backgrounds With Boomerang Kids." PhD diss., Walden University.

36 Tsilimparis, John. 2012. "7 Tips for Parents to Manage Empty Nest Syndrome." *Huffington Post,* July 27, 2012. https://www.huffpost.com/entry/empty-nest_b_1710478.

37 Crawford, Joan. 2017. *My Way of Life*. Los Angeles: Graymalkin Media, p. 79.

38 Dunbar, Paul Laurence. 1997. *Lyrics of Lowly Life: The Poetry of Paul Laurence Dunbar*. New York: Carol Publishing Group, pp. 61–65.

39 Middleton, Kate. 2017. "The Launch of the 'Out of the Blue' Film Series with Best Beginnings and Heads Together." Filmed March 2017 at the Royal College of Obstetricians and Gynaecologists, London, UK. Video, 5:11. https://www.royal.uk/speech-duchess-cambridge-best-beginnings-out-blue-film-series-launch.

40 Bahr, Anna. 2014. "When the College Admissions Battle Starts at Age 3." *New York Times*, July 29, 2014. https://www.nytimes.com/2014/07/30/upshot/when-the-college-admissions-battle-starts-at-age-3.html.

41 Marian, Viorica, and Anthony Shook. "The Cognitive Benefits of Being Bilingual." *Cerebrum: The Dana Forum on Brain Science*, vol. 2012 (2012): 13.

42 The Vanguard Corporation. n.d. "When Should You Start Saving for College?" Accessed October 22, 2020. https://investor.vanguard.com/college-savings-plans/when-to-start.

43 Brown, Brené. 2012. "The Wholehearted Parenting Manifesto," *HuffPost: The Blog*, September 28, updated November 28, 2012. Accessed March 23, 2020. https://www.huffpost.com/entry/wholehearted-parenting-manifesto_b_1923011.

CPSIA information can be obtained
at www.ICGtesting.com
Printed in the USA
BVHW031550230321
603273BV00015B/842/J